Yards of Purple

STORIES FOR ADVENT

yards *of* purple

SARAH M. FOULGER

United Church Press

Cleveland, Ohio

United Church Press, Cleveland, Ohio 44115
© 1999 by Sarah M. Foulger

Biblical quotations are from the New Revised Standard Version of
the Bible, © 1989 by the Division of Christian Education of the
National Council of the Churches of Christ in the U.S.A., and are
used by permission. Adapted for inclusivity.

Printed in the United States of America on acid-free paper

04 03 02 01 00 99   5 4 3 2 1

Library of Congress Cataloging-in-Publication Data

Foulger, Sarah M. (Sarah Marguerite), 1955–
    Yards of purple : stories for Advent / Sarah M. Foulger.
      p.   cm.
    Includes index.
    ISBN 0-8298-1312-8 (pbk. : alk. paper)
    1. Advent—Meditations.   I. Title.
BV40.F68   1999
242'.332—dc21   98-50325
                                              CIP

For Russell, Noah, and Christopher,

my extraordinary family,

and for the wonderful people of the churches I have served.

Thanks be to God,

whose love, imagination, and wit sustain me.

Contents

Introduction

*A*dvent is a season of preparation for the incarnation, a time of preparing our hearts for the birth of the Christ child. It is also a wonderful season for storytelling. There is no shortage of amazing Christmas tales. However, many of the available stories are either quite secular in nature or specifically geared for younger children. The following stories are intended to be used by adults and older children as a way of preparing hearts and urging thoughtfulness during Advent. Twelve of them are prompted by the lectionary lessons designated for the Sundays during each of the three cycles of Advent. The thirteenth story is inspired by the lectionary lessons for Christmas Eve.

This book may be used by individuals or families who are seeking to explore the meaning of Advent and Christmas. I hope it will also be employed by congregations as an Advent study tool. The book offers three years' worth of Advent study material. At the end of each story, you will find a list of questions for reflection and discussion. Three of the Advent stories were first presented as sermons, and all may be used in this way. I highly recommend a thoughtful review of the related scripture lessons before reading each story. This will add life and depth to your reading and reflection.

These are all contemporary stories about very different kinds of individuals, each of whom is struggling with an issue such as freedom, responsibility, repentance, or the presence of God. All of the characters described herein are fictional. However, there are, here and there, bits and pieces of autobiographical material. Also, several of the stories, such as the one about the elevator, are loosely based on situations that I and others have actually experienced. It is my sincerest hope that you both enjoy and find meaning in these short adventures. May God bless you as you prepare, once more, for the wonderful gift of the incarnation.

Miracle Cookies

Isaiah 2:1–5, Matthew 24:36–44

—

God shall judge between the nations, and shall arbitrate
for many peoples; they shall beat their swords into
plowshares, and their spears into pruning hooks; nation
shall not lift up sword against nation, neither shall they
learn war any more.

🕊 Isaiah 2:4

Keep awake therefore, for you do not know on what day
your God is coming.

🕊 Matthew 24:42

*J*anine Harris was afflicted by all manner of social infirmity.
She was an unemployed, middle-aged, poor woman with high
blood pressure. She lived in a dump of a building in a complex that
was designated for folks in her impoverished situation. And most
painful of all, she was suffering from empty-nest syndrome. Janine
had only one child, Seretha, now in her junior year of college on the
other side of the country. She had done her best to raise Seretha on
her own, and while she knew that Seretha's education in such a far-
away place meant that both of them had succeeded, she missed her

beautiful daughter "something awful." Seretha called her mother at least once a week, and each call inevitably led to a discussion about Janine's safety. Seretha was justifiably concerned for her mother's future.

The biggest problem in the neighborhood these days was gang violence. Janine was afraid to leave the apartment except in the middle of the day. Even then she watched her back closely. In fact, she watched a great deal. Resting her bony elbows on the cracked Formica kitchen counter, Janine often peered between the top and bottom of her pale yellow café curtains, keeping a lookout for danger. Too often was she caught between feeling angry at the gun-toting kids in her apartment complex and feeling utterly sorry for them. What kind of a life did they have? They were even more trapped by neighborhood violence than she was. Kids associated with gangs had to watch their backs with an even greater vigilance.

Janine wondered what had gone wrong with the world. Why, when so many had fought so long and hard for freedom, are so many kids bound by poverty and violence? Why are they chained to forces so destructive that there are no adequate names for them? Why do these kids have so much free time that they do not know what to do with themselves? Why are they angry at each other when there are plenty of other folks in the world far more deserving of that hostility? Why, some two thousand years after the birth of the gentle Savior, is there no peace? Can a way be cleared through this terrible mess?

Three months ago, in the middle of a breezeless, golden autumn day, a ten-year-old boy on the next block was gunned down by a bunch of kids driving by in a stolen car. Janine knew him: Michael. She had known Michael from the time he was a toddler. She knew his mother, May, and his younger sister, Leslie. May was a good mother, Janine thought. The terrible truth was that the power of the streets was greater than that of most mothers. "There but for the grace of God," she mumbled to herself. Michael was, according to investigators, a member of the gang that called itself "Rage." The kids in the

car were members of a rival gang calling themselves "Smoke." There
were retaliations and counter-retaliations, tires slashed, faces slashed,
bullets removed from muscle-bound arms and shattered kneecaps.
Many of the kids in Janine's immediate neighborhood were members
of Rage. Janine was glad that Seretha had, by virtue of brains, determination, and divine providence, made it out. And as much as Janine
missed her baby girl, she hoped Seretha would not have to come back
into this scrap of a place or any other like it.

Janine did her best with her meager space. She kept it clean and
polished and sprayed for persistent bugs. Right now it was decorated
for Christmas. There was no tree yet, but there were lots of fresh
greens. Every year, her neighbor Jim drove up to New England,
brought back a truckload of freshly cut fir trees, and sold them from
the corner of a car lot downtown. There were always odd trees left
over by Christmas Eve, trees with crooked trunks or sparse branches
or big bald spots, and Jim would bring one by for her. Early in the
season, he also supplied her with a big bag full of trimmed branches,
which she used to make the place more alive in a gloomy season.

Janine had saved every Christmas ornament Seretha ever made,
from the construction-paper chains (now faded in color yet brighter
in love), to raggedy-looking Santas constructed of Styrofoam balls
with felt hats and glued cotton beards, to Bethlehem stars fashioned
of paper plates and glitter. These treasures were proudly displayed on
the windowsills around the apartment. She kept Advent candles surrounded by fragrant greens in the middle of her kitchen table. These
she would light once a week throughout the season of Advent, offering prayers for all the folks she knew who needed them. Today
marked the lighting of the first candle.

In addition to these festive touches, this afternoon the place was
filled with the warm, sweet smell of sugar cookies. The third batch
was now in the oven. These were no ordinary cookies. They were
peace cookies, filled with warm hopes and courageous dreams.
Janine tried to keep her well-developed skepticism far from the

making of them. For today, something miraculous was going to
happen—she hoped, everyone hoped. It was, in fact, a miracle that
the whole project had come this far. And her extraordinary cookies
held an honored place in the momentous design.

The miracle started when one old man, who lived three blocks
away from Janine on the edge of Smoke territory, woke up one day
and decided that enough was enough. He was tired of being afraid.
He was tired of reading about dead and wounded neighbors in the
newspaper. He was tired of living in a virtual war zone. And he had
been tired of it since he himself was a kid. Janine did not know
his first name. Everybody called him "Old Man Williams." Williams
and another senior citizen named Owens joined forces and decided
to try to bring the violence to an end. So Williams and Owens met
with the leaders of both gangs and organized a shaky truce. Now,
after nearly three months of working with these kids—often one on
one—today was treaty day. The treaty itself was a collaborative effort.
The signing was going to take place in the fellowship hall of the big
Baptist church. Janine's cookies were being baked by special request
and would be an important part of the postsigning celebration.

When Williams was a kid, he belonged to a gang called "the
Ravens." The big rival gang of his day was called "the Rockets."
Williams had a good friend, Isaiah, who went off and joined the
Rockets, bringing the friendship to a bitter and nearly tragic end.
During one terrible midsummer face-off, Isaiah stabbed him in the
back, quite literally. Fortunately for Williams, no major organs were
struck. But the friendship, which both kids had been trying to hang
on to in spite of their separate gangs, was irrevocably broken. Old
Man Williams had never forgiven his childhood buddy.

Curiously enough, Williams and Isaiah Owens, now in their sev-
enties, lived only six blocks apart. Williams had thought about that
fact more and more as he watched the raw gang violence escalate.
The hatred, the rivalry, the internalization of oppression, were the
same now as they had been in his own Ravens days. But the weapons

had changed. Kids had greater access to guns that were more sophisticated and deadly than ever. On the morning when little Michael
was shot, Williams decided he could not hide anymore from what
was happening all around him. With a will to forgive and the kernel
of an idea, he walked the six long blocks to Owens's apartment
building and resumed a friendship that had faltered almost sixty
years ago.

How much they held in common after all that time was nothing
short of remarkable. They had both served in the army. They had
both worked for the city—one a janitor, the other a sanitation engi-
neer. They had both maintained an interest in jazz music. Each was
in pretty good physical shape for his age. They were both disgusted
and frustrated by the turmoil in the neighborhood. They were both
stubbornly alone. When Williams told his old adversary and friend
that he wanted to try to put an end to the bloodshed, Owens was
ready to join forces. They tossed around some bold thoughts and
decided that if they were ever going to pull this thing off, they
needed help.

Owens and Williams had been meeting now for three months,
along with ten other concerned senior citizens whom they had
enlisted in their plan. The group was called SIP, short for "Swords
into Plowshares," and Owens and Williams gallantly shared the lead-
ership. SIP devised a brave plan—a plan that would take a lot of
work, a lot of commitment, an unknown quantity of risk, and as
much neighborhood support as they could muster. The most important components of the plan turned out to be the trusting relationships that developed between gang members and SIP leaders. The
second most important component was letting the kids themselves
come up with ideas—ideas like peer counseling, a safe zone, a community center, and a "guns-for-gift-certificates" swap.

Much of what SIP expected to happen did, in fact, take place. For
example, there was a great deal of resistance. Hatred is a fiercely contagious virus, not easily slowed in its course. At first, SIP members

received threatening phone calls and ugly graffiti messages. But Owens and Williams fearlessly shared their own story over and over again until the power of forgiveness became irresistible. There were some interesting surprises along the way, too. There was the day, for instance, when Isaiah asked one of the Rage leaders, a tall string bean of a kid called Bullet, why he did the things he did, and Bullet said, "You know, nobody ever asked me that before." A thoughtfulness was working its way through the neighborhood.

A recently retired teacher and SIP member, Edmund Lockhart, who lived just outside of gang territory but wanted to become involved anyway, became a mentor to three of the kids who were not yet teenagers but were firmly attached to gangs. Gangs took the place of family for many members whose parents were unavailable to them for a variety of reasons: some parents were drug abusers; some were incarcerated; some single parents worked two or three minimum-wage jobs in order to pay the bills. For these three boys, Edmund became a combination surrogate grandfather, coach, teacher, and friend. They ate most dinners together now and shot hoops when the weather cooperated. As it turned out, Edmund was a not-too-shabby free thrower. While it might have felt like a burden to some, Edmund Lockhart was having the time of his life with these kids.

When they heard what was going on, local businesses wanted in on the action. An old pizza restaurant owned by a third-generation Italian family, which despite the violence stubbornly refused to turn tail and move their business out of the neighborhood, donated pies every time there was a meeting. A Cambodian grocer offered two gallons of apple cider to go with the pizza each time. A Jewish garment merchant gave SIP one hundred T-shirts printed with a logo that one of the Smoke members had designed. A local sporting-goods store donated two new basketball hoops, which were installed in an empty lot in the safe zone. Local politicians wanted a piece of the miracle, but SIP steadfastly refused to become anything more or less than a neighborhood uprising.

Janine was not an SIP member. She had not been involved in any of the planning, and she fully intended to continue maintaining a safe distance from anyone she thought might be related to a gang. But having heard about the amazing doings, she prayed for them all: SIP members, gang members, perpetrators, victims, the whole neighborhood. And when she received the phone call asking her to bake some of her famous sugar cookies for the treaty celebration, she was glad to do it. She bought special red and green sugar crystals with which to decorate them later. Everything about the preparation of these cookies entailed extra care on Janine's part. She had even tried to form the dough into the shape of doves, but they baked into blobby-looking creatures, and she went back to the good old-fashioned round version.

When they were all baked, Janine called Leslie, little Michael's grieving sister, and asked her if she would like to come over and decorate her peace cookies. Leslie was a little hesitant but, in the end, was lured by the promise that in addition to being the chief icing spreader and sugar crystal operator, she could also be in charge of quality control. Janine was grateful that since her own little girl was gone, there were still plenty of little girls in the neighborhood to borrow. She knew Seretha would approve. When the cookies were finished, Janine and Leslie stood back and admired their handiwork. Then they each selected one for the tasting. Janine and Leslie agreed that they were ready for delivery.

Now, nobody who had lived through as much as Old Man Williams, Isaiah Owens, and Edmund Lockhart (and Janine Harris, for that matter) held any illusions about the truce between gangs. Knowing well the clay matter and rough edges and short fuses of humanity, they knew this could well be a miracle with limitations. Leslie asked, "Do you think this treaty is really gonna work?" Janine answered with an optimistic lilt in her voice, "Who knows? I think it just might. Who knows?" Allowing the splendid smell of the miracle cookies to fill her senses, Janine considered the fallout of love, the redemptive power of forgiveness, the magnificence of living in community, and the immeasurable impact of God's judgment. She reiterated, "Who but God Almighty knows!" and gave Leslie a big hug.

Questions for Reflection and Discussion

1. Do you hold anything in common with Janine Harris? With Old Man Williams or Isaiah Owens? In what way is your life most different from theirs?
2. Are there dangers in your life? What are they? How do you handle them? What else can be done about them?
3. What are the specific problems in your neighborhood? What can be done to help remedy these?
4. What was the first step Old Man Williams took in initiating the process of forgiveness?
5. Why do kids join gangs?
6. What do you think happened in the neighborhood after the truce? Did it last?
7. Can you name or imagine ways in which contemporary swords can be transformed into plowshares?
8. Janine's cookies were put to work in a special way. Think of ordinary things that may be divinely employed in extraordinary ways.

Worthy of Repentance

Isaiah 11:1–10, Matthew 3:1–12

—

Righteousness shall be the belt around his waist, and faithfulness the belt around his loins.

⇒ Isaiah 11:5

But when John the Baptist saw many Pharisees and Sadducees coming for baptism, he said to them, "You brood of vipers! Who warned you to flee from the wrath to come? Bear fruit worthy of repentance."

⇒ Matthew 3:7–8

John had lost almost everything: his dignity; his self-respect; and, most grievously, his long-suffering wife, Allison, and his precious daughter, Elizabeth. Lizzie was now eleven. She was just nine when Allison kicked John out of the house once and for all. Lizzie's faith, however, had walked out on him long ago, after years of living with the frightful stranger who emerged when John had a bellyful of alcohol.

Every night, as long as Lizzie could remember, her daddy came home from work quietly grumpy, went off into the den with a glass and a bottle of something, usually Scotch, and became progressively more vicious. He never hit Lizzie or Allison. No. That almost would have been easier for them to understand. His weapons were not his fists, but rather his words—words cruelly flung mainly at her mother, but often enough at Lizzie, too.

The divorce went through over John's pallid objections. At the time, he was privately furious. He had even banged a hole in the bedroom wall with the side of his hand. He had not understood why everyone but his own father was taking Allison's side. Now he knew. Now he understood. He would carry the burden of his drunken monstrousness for the rest of his (by the grace of God) sober life.

Fortunately, his job remained intact. He was an actuary with an old New England insurance company. His drinking had tiptoed lightly through the office, causing an occasional late arrival. None of his colleagues guessed what happened after he left work. They knew him as a quiet, hard-working employee who crunched numbers with the best of them, ate his bag lunch alone, and managed to get through the office doors on time most mornings. Oh, the signs were there: bleary eyes, pink nose, a slight shakiness. No one noticed, however. And no one had any idea that John Abramson went home and drank himself into a stupor most nights.

He had been sober now for almost six months, since June 24, a date that would long remain in his encumbered memory. On that evening six months ago, more than a year after the divorce and with eight beers from a local brew pub under his belt, John Abramson got into his car, headed to his little apartment, and hit a dog—a small, brownish, curly-haired mutt that had anticipated a zig where the speeding John had zagged. In an instant, the dog was badly injured. Neighbors who heard the screeching car witnessed the whole pitiful event and called the police right away.

And that was it—John's moment of truth. None of the staring neighbors, who seemed as ghosts to John, knew where the dog belonged. It was taken to a nearby vet. Broken ribs, internal bleeding, and a crushed right front paw were the initial diagnoses. After the accident, during John's first few chilling days of sobriety, he checked on the little dog every day. He placed an ad in the local paper, but no one came forward to claim him. So, when the dog dared to recover, John paid the bill, took him home, and named him Trooper.

Trooper was all-forgiving but would, for the rest of his life, bear a memorial limp. The limp would forever remind John of a small boy, perhaps six or seven years of age, who emerged from the faceless crowd gathered at the scene of the accident. The boy knelt next to Trooper like an angel, stroking the abject creature's uninjured head with great love. Once he looked up at John with great condemning eyes, which continued to haunt him.

He could do nothing to blot out the pain he had both caused and witnessed. With this event, the seriousness of his drinking problem became decisively and overwhelmingly evident. By the grace of God, in whom he now believed as never before, and with the support of total strangers he had come to know in detox and beyond, John stopped drinking. For one day at a time—sometimes one minute at a time—he stayed sober. He harbored no delusions. He knew Allison would never take him back, and he did not blame her in any way for kicking him out. He had not seen Lizzie since the divorce was finalized. Not that he was avoiding her. No, it was Lizzie who refused to see him. He hoped, though, that he could somehow prove his trustworthiness to Lizzie or, at the very least, do something good for her.

In his imagination, he pictured a Christmas dinner, in his own small apartment and cooked by himself: an apricot-glazed turkey, mashed potatoes with savory gravy, cranberry-orange relish, pumpkin pie. He wanted both of them to see him sober, to see that he could be kind to them. During the past year, Allison had started a successful but demanding catering business. A Christmas dinner that she did not have to cook might appeal to her. John had become a fairly good cook himself, especially in the past six months. He had

Second Sunday, Year A

even taken two cooking classes offered at a local health food store and learned to make some dishes that were as difficult to spell as they were to prepare. He was the only man who signed up for these classes, but he hung in there, using Trooper as an eager guinea pig for his early culinary disasters.

There would be gifts at this dream dinner, not for the purpose of buying their affection but to show them he still cared. For years they had listened to his short-lived promises and swallowed his insults even as they had cleaned up his messes. He wanted to show them he was a changed man, a changing man. He looked over in the corner at Trooper, who, curled up in the comfort of his little bed, thumped his tail in delight at the attentive glance.

Today—this very morning, December 10—John Abramson summoned his courage and dialed his ex-wife's phone number, which was, in fact, his old home number. He reached an answering machine and listened as his daughter's monotone voice said, "I'm sorry but we can't take your call right now. Please leave a message." Her voice still carried the weight of the world in it. He wished with all his heart that he could go back and give her some joy in those early years. He took a deep breath and said, "Hi. This is John . . . uh, this is Daddy, Lizzie. I'm calling to invite you and your mother here for dinner on Christmas Day. I hope you will consider my invitation. Please let me know." He thought about adding "I love you," but had used those words so often in his weak morning-after apologies that he was afraid the words would sound hollow. He would have to demonstrate his love in whatever ways they might now permit him. If they would permit him—a big "if." "Please, dear God, oh please," he prayed in a whisper as he returned the receiver to its cradle. Trooper uttered some guttural noise, which, for all the world, sounded like an "amen." "What would I do without you?" John uttered to his furry companion.

The embers of his faint hope fanned, John stared at his little kitchen table and daydreamed about a white tablecloth and napkins and candles and goblets, none of which he owned. He decided to go shopping for those things right away. Though it felt early for shopping, 10:28 according to the digital alarm clock on his kitchen counter, he felt certain that the local variety store opened at 11:00 on Sundays. Readying himself with a fleece-lined jacket, John grabbed his keys and told a disappointed Trooper to hold the fort while he was gone. Trooper loved walks and seemed unbothered by his withered paw. "We'll go for a walk later," he offered reassuringly.

It was cold out—a damp, raw cold—but his quick pace and his Christmas dream warmed him. He had grown accustomed to walking in the weeks during which his license was revoked and in the early months of learning how to be a dog owner. Never having owned any sort of pet before, it was all new to him, the flea thing, the heartworm thing, the inappropriate scratching thing, veterinary responsibilities, feeding and watering and walking responsibilities, scooping responsibilities. He used dozens of nicknames for his adopted friend: Lefty, Sherlock, Bruiser, Ahab, Knievel. The unjustifiably grateful dog answered to all of them.

John passed rows of quiet homes. He passed the bicycle shop and the antique store. With each block, the familiar streets became less residential. He passed the corner where the Methodist and Episcopal churches faced each other like two friends unable to leave each other's side. John was not a churchgoer. His mother had called herself a "home Baptist," and his father, who claimed both Jewish and Catholic backgrounds, called himself a secular humanist. As an adult, he knew how to define those terms. As a child, however, he had known exactly what they meant: They meant he did not have to go to church. He was now glad for the existence of religious institutions and their good works, but he was not ready to step into one. He had found a congregation among the recovering, and supposed that someday he might try slipping into a back pew somewhere. But not today.

Each church on this particular corner had a sign, the message of which changed each week. He looked forward to reading them on this frequently traveled route. The Methodist church sign currently read, "Jesus Is the Reason for the Season." The Episcopal sign read, "Bear Fruits Worthy of Repentance." The latter seemed an odd message for the Christmas season. Nevertheless, it seemed a personal message to him and exactly what he needed to do at this point in his life: bear fruits worthy of repentance. It was not enough to have repented; he must now maintain his repentance, thoughtfully declare it, steadfastly defend it. He must be a repented person. He dare not advertise his repentance, but rather he must struggle to live it.

John heard music coming from the packed Methodist church and crept closer. Standing beneath one window, he heard many voices singing, "O come, O come, Emmanuel, and ransom captive Israel, that mourns in lonely exile here." He knew what it meant: Emmanuel, God with us. "God be with Lizzie," he prayed in the silence of his heart, "God be with all of us who mourn in lonely exile here."

He reached his destination, a small local establishment, owned by the same family for more than forty years, a shop that had a little bit of everything in it. He glanced down at his watch: 11:08. As John had hoped, the shop was open. He took a moment to drink in the Christmas feel that had been carefully draped and hung and hot-glued together for another season. Paper snowflakes hung from threads attached to the ceiling tiles. Proudly displayed in the center of the store stood a large artificial tree covered with shiny red ribbons and crowded by tastefully wrapped but certainly empty boxes.

John headed in the direction of what looked to be the housewares section, where he was interrupted by an eager young saleswoman soliciting his wishes. There were no other customers, and, while he would normally find such interference bothersome, today he was grateful for the help. Shopping was not high on his list of favorite pastimes, and housewares other than pots and pans were largely foreign objects to him. He reviewed his list with the saleswoman, and she helped him choose a lovely ivory tablecloth with a partridge-in-a-pear-tree pattern woven into the fabric. She talked him into four of everything, even though he needed just three: four matching napkins, four gold-ringed water goblets, four lords-a-leaping linen placemats, four swans-a-swimming napkin rings, four china plates with ladies dancing and maids-a-milking and pipers piping delicately adorning the edges, and finally, two turtledove candlesticks.

The stash filled two large Christmas shopping bags festooned on both sides with enormous laughing Santas. Santa appeared, for all the world, to be laughing directly at him. He did feel a little silly with all this theme-driven dinnerware but remained convinced that, however ridiculous, it would be pleasing to Lizzie.

Back home again, he unwrapped everything and set the table as Trooper watched with interest. When he was finished, it looked more like a miniature theme park than a kitchen table. He leaned back against the kitchen counter, staring in amazement at the whole distinctively festive picture for the longest time. Finally, he said, "What do you think, Rudolph?" Trooper wiggled approvingly and scratched at the door. As if he were talking to a baby, John babbled, "You gotta go out, Bouncer? Of course you do."

While John was outside with the greatly relieved Trooper, the phone rang. Lizzie reciprocated an answering machine message, "Thanks for the invitation, Dad. Mom and I, well . . . we'll think about it and . . . get back to you. See ya." When they returned and retrieved the message, John, who had been holding his breath while he listened, smiled broadly and said to his little buddy, "They didn't say 'no.' They didn't say 'no.'" His friend limped over to him and licked his hand. "I can't ask for much more than that," he continued. "Maybe they'll give me a chance—God did, you did, maybe they will." He let out a sigh of longing and then another sigh loaded with unarticulated thanks: thanks for an advent of repentance, thanks for the strength to bear fruits worthy of that repentance, and thanks for hope itself in every one of its miraculous forms.

Second Sunday, Year A

Questions for Reflection and Discussion

1. John's moment of truth occurred when he hit Trooper with his car. What moments of truth can you identify in your life?
2. What role did the little boy at the scene of the accident play? When is it appropriate to render judgment?
3. What did John want most from his family? What do you want most from your family? What was John most able to offer his family? What are your gifts to your family?
4. Does John deserve his family's trust? Is there evidence that he may be trusted? Have you ever broken a trust or had one broken? How did this feel?
5. In what ways is the hand of God visible in this story?
6. Why did the sign at the Episcopal church strike John so? Is it possible to maintain repentance? How?
7. Will all of the "things" John purchased help his situation? If so, how? If not, why not?
8. Do you think John's family will accept his invitation to Christmas dinner?

An Unexpected Blooming

Isaiah 35:1–10, Matthew 11:2–11

—

The wilderness and the dry land shall be glad, the desert shall rejoice and blossom. . . . Strengthen the weak hands, and make firm the feeble knees. Say to those who are of a fearful heart, "Be strong, do not fear!"

⤳ Isaiah 35:1, 3, 4a

Jesus answered John's disciples, "Go and tell John what you hear and see: the blind receive their sight, the lame walk, the lepers are cleansed, the deaf hear, the dead are raised, and the poor have good news brought to them."

⤳ Matthew 11:4–5

Her parents held high hopes for a daughter of great elegance, a feminine reflection of her distinguished European background. They named her Johanna Marie. It became apparent, however, within the first two years of her being, that she was a Johnny—a tree-climbing, hot-tempered, insect-loving tomboy, now aged into an odd old lady. She was at least a little crazy, and she knew

17

it. When she was nineteen, a stuffy little psychiatrist told her parents it was a touch of schizophrenia. The husband to whom she was married for twenty-seven grueling months had called her much worse than that. He was no prince, but she suspected that most of his insults were somewhat justifiable. "I thank my lucky stars there were no kids!" she repeated many times after the divorce. Often she felt that those were the only lucky stars that would ever shine down from her disproportionately unlucky universe.

Johnny spent most of her life alone, an unattractive misfit, struggling to make a place for herself in a world of norms too narrow for the likes of her. When her ungratified mother died eighteen years ago, three years after her father left to meet his Maker, Johnny moved back into their big Victorian house, the very house into which she was born. The neighborhood had suffered some changes in her eighty-seven years. For a while, it deteriorated. Then it started to gentrify. Now it was a real upper-crust sort of place again, much as it had been when Johnny was a little girl. The homes around her sported minor improvements, a sunroom here, a skylight there. The trees remained familiar but larger, gnarlier. She knew them well, having climbed most of them. They were her observation towers, safe places from which to watch from a distance the other neighborhood children who were so very normal, from their game-playing to their vicious cruelties. Her parents tried for many years to encourage the other children to accept Johnny, but their efforts were painfully unsuccessful.

There were not so many children on the block these days, but there were plenty of young professionals interested in bettering their real estate investments. Recent neighborhood improvements included Victorian-style lampposts, weathered brick sidewalks, a "no lawn ornaments" policy, and, for the Christmas season, "the candle plan." The candle plan was the brainchild of Johnny's new neighbors to the right, Forrest and Suzanne Goring ("rhymes with boring," Johnny told her pet finches). Forrest and Suzanne were both attorneys. "Well, aren't they the cutest pair of bloodsuckers," she mused to her beloved feathered friends.

The candle plan required all of the residents of this historic area of town to place a white candle in each window of their lovely old homes during the month of December. The candles were to be removed on New Year's Day. These pristine candles, according to the Gorings, would turn the entire neighborhood into the picture of traditional Christmas charm. Johnny, because she could not imagine being a part of what she considered to be a scheme to gild the neighborhood, refused to comply. Furthermore, she had bought a big plastic reindeer with a lightbulb in it at a yard sale last summer and put it right in the middle of the yard. She intended to leave it there until spring. She was not trying to be different; she simply *was* different.

Her eyes wandered from the horrid glowing reindeer back to the trees. They were now gray and lifeless hibernators, closed for the season. At the top of the old crabapple in her front yard, Johnny spied three brown leaves clinging tenaciously to an otherwise bare branch. It was after two in the afternoon, and she thought she should probably eat something—not that she was hungry, mind you, but she was determined to keep up her strength in old age. She planned on living at least another seven years. If anything happened to her, who would care for the birds?

Johnny had a family of golden finches, five of them. She allowed them to fly freely through the house, and she kept a supply of Lysol at the ready for daily cleanup. She believed that birds were not nearly as messy as most people thought. They were lovely and graceful and perfectly at home as birds. They balanced the household, she felt, for she was awkward and clumsy and could not figure how best to be human.

She wondered often what it means to be human: Is it all about struggling and mourning and feeling humiliated and then, if you are lucky, watching your hands grow stiff and your knees turn feeble and buying finch food by the peck? As she continued to stare out of what was called the "keeping room" window, Johnny saw smoke. At first it was just a little, and she thought it curious that the Gorings had a fire going. They were not usually home during the day. The smoke did not appear to be coming from a chimney although it was difficult to tell because that house had four chimneys, fairly evenly spaced on the rooftop. When she saw flames suddenly shoot from the roof, she knew all was not well with the distinguished firm of Goring and Goring.

Johnny went looking for the phone book, and, finding it on top of her refrigerator, she searched for the emergency phone number, the pained knots in her hands complaining as she looked for the listing. As soon as she located the number, she realized that she had known it all along. She stopped short of calling when she heard the sirens and soon after, watched the frenzied arrival of the big yellow-green trucks. Firefighters set to work with great energy to contain the fire. The house went up, however, like a matchstick, for its timbers were old and dry. The firefighters busied themselves hosing down nearby roofs and trees.

Johnny knew this was a terrible tragedy. She could not help but think, however, that the fire was quite beautiful in its rich coloring and passionate determination. It was dreadful, yet somehow magnificent, and it was certainly powerful. She could feel the heat of it even from inside her own home, and she knew, from their sudden frenetic energy, that her dear little birds could feel it, too.

She watched as the Gorings arrived in separate cars. She saw Forrest trying to comfort his inconsolable wife in the midst of a great deal of smoke and confusion. Johnny felt very awkward doing it, but she donned her shabby old brown woolen coat and a very goofy-looking but warm aviator hat she had picked up at a flea market and walked over to where the Gorings were holding fast to one another in the street.

Each step was difficult for her. It was like coming down from one of her trees and approaching some of the other children. She realized that she did not need her coat and hat, because while the weather was near freezing, the air was hot and filled with smoke. "Excuse me," she said in her most polite voice, "would you like to come in and sit down?" She pointed to her home. Through a twisted and tear-streaked face, Suzanne thanked Johnny but told her they should really stay until the firefighters were finished.

One of the firefighters, who was standing nearby taking a breather, overheard the offer. He told the Gorings that they would be better off inside. He practically insisted the Gorings go with Johnny and told them he would come and find them when it was all over. In their current state of imposed vulnerability, they followed Johnny into her house, where she took the distraught neighbors' coats and seated them on a lumpy old loveseat. The house was clean but strange. The Gorings were too forlorn to notice anything about it, even as the friendliest of the finches flew over and sat on the fireplace mantel across from the loveseat to assess the intruders. Johnny asked them if they would like some tea or prune juice, and they numbly accepted the tea suggestion. Johnny thought they looked utterly spent.

She filled the tea kettle and located three mugs in a kitchen cabinet. Then she returned them to their appointed shelf and went into the dining room, where she removed three lovely teacups and saucers from a beautiful mahogany china closet. These she rinsed off and set aside. She went back for the matching teapot and cleaned that out, too. She looked through the pantry, hoping to find a package of cookies, but there was none. Then she remembered an unopened box of Christmas ribbon candy that she had bought last year during the postseason clearance sales. Candy like that did not go bad, did it? She found the box on a shelf in her own bedroom closet and was pleased to have remembered not only that she had it but where she had left it. Johnny arranged some of the candy in a cut-glass bowl and placed everything on a tray. Just as she was pulling three linen napkins from a drawer, she heard the tea kettle whistle; she let the hot water run over three Red Rose tea bags into the china pot. As she

carried the tray into the living room, Johnny realized that her hands
had not bothered her at all during these preparations. Her knees
seemed to have new life in them.

Before she reached the living room, she heard a knock at the door.
Johnny set the tray down on a side table in the keeping room and
went to answer it. A lovely-looking young woman, who looked to be
in her early forties, stood on her stoop holding a plate laden with
cookies—oatmeal, Johnny thought. The woman had an odd look on
her face but not one that was unfamiliar to Johnny. She seemed to
evoke such faces. It was then, before a word had passed between them,
that Johnny realized she was still wearing her coat and beloved hat.

Not just anyone could wear a brown leather aviator's hat—only
mavericks, only the most courageous, only those who were willing to
fly in the face of convention. Though they had never met, Amelia
Earhart felt like a friend to Johnny. She understood Amelia in all her
differentness, and she was glad for Amelia's successes. Johnny was
seventeen when Amelia Earhart made her first transatlantic flight.
Her father, knowing well Johnny's almost obsessive interest, gave her
a signed copy of Earhart's book for her eighteenth birthday. She still
had it, and continued to treasure it. Amelia Earhart disappeared
almost one month after Johnny's wedding. This, Johnny knew, was
some sort of terrible sign. Long after her probable death, Amelia
remained a defiant symbol of hope to Johnny and proof that it is
possible for a nonconformist to make a place for herself in the world.

The young woman interrupted Johnny's thoughts with a softly
spoken, "Hello. My name is Loreen. I understand the Gorings are
here. May I come in?"

"By all means. Do come in. Do come in." She removed her hat
and stuffed as much of it as she could into her coat pocket.

"We haven't met before, have we?"

From her daily detailed observations, Johnny felt as if she knew
most of her nearby neighbors quite well. She had never actually met

them, however, and she was not prepared to like any of them as much as she liked this woman from the start.

"And what may I call you, Miss . . . ?"

"Oh, Johnny—call me Johnny, plain old Johnny. The Gorings are in there." Awkwardly taking the plate of cookies from Loreen, she motioned her around the corner to the living room.

Johnny replaced the ribbon candy on the tray with the fresh cookies. She removed her own coat and hung it on an empty hook near the front door. Then she fetched the tray and carried it in to where three of her neighbors now sat. Suzanne Goring seemed to be reciting a litany of all the possessions that most concerned her. While Johnny expected the litany to be full of priceless clocks and designer clothes, the list contained all of the items Johnny would also be most disturbed to lose: photographs, a baptismal gown that had been in her family for several generations and which she hoped to use for her own baby's christening when she and Forrest were ready to have a child, a beautifully hand-lettered poem that her father had written and framed for her—all items that were worth little or nothing on the market but were truly priceless to Suzanne. Perhaps this young woman was not as selfish and trend driven as Johnny thought.

She poured tea for her three guests and was holding out the plate of cookies, explaining that Loreen had brought them over, when there was yet another knock at the door. While many homeowners are accustomed to regular knocks at their doors, this was a banner day in Johnny's life. The only people who knocked at Johnny's door now were the letter carrier and the oil-delivery worker. Johnny never answered when they knocked; she pretended not to be home, and later in the day gathered up whatever they had left. Here she was, answering the door for the second time within a few short minutes. A young man with a teenage daughter stood at the door. This time Johnny started the introductions. "Hello. My name is Johnny, and you are the people who live diagonally across the street, are you not?"

⌒
Third Sunday, Year A

Johnny did not take after her parents in very many ways, but, like them, she knew how to be gracious.

Johnny invited Bob Gunther and his daughter Faith into the living room and left to retrieve more teacups. Shirley Gunther arrived a few minutes later, carrying a basket of fruit. Within the hour, Johnny was hosting a group of seventeen neighbors who wanted to offer support to the Gorings. Food arrived in a steady stream: vegetables with dip, almond cookies, eggnog. Neighbors had divided themselves into little groups. The finches made themselves scarce. At one point, Forrest Goring laughed out loud, suggesting that except for the burning building, this was the best Christmas party to which they had ever been invited in this neighborhood.

Johnny ended up spending most of her time with Faith Gunther, who was, apparently, starting a junior-year honors project researching the history of her historic neighborhood. She found Johnny to be a tremendous resource and talked her into setting up several interviews. The neighbors were much friendlier up close than Johnny ever imagined they would be. They seemed to be enjoying their odd old neighbor. Thankfully, no one said a word about the reindeer, which Johnny was sure had suffered so much smoke damage by now that it would have to be dispatched to the dump.

It was unquestionably a difficult season for the Gorings, who went to live with Forrest's mother while the house was completely rebuilt. It was, however, a season of unexpected blossoming for Johnny— Johnny the sudden hostess, Johnny the neighborhood historian. For the first time in her life and in a time of seasonal austerity, she felt warm earth surround her roots.

Questions for Reflection and Discussion

1. How does it happen that someone becomes a misfit? Who sets the parameters of "normal"?
2. Is there anything Johnny's parents could have done to help her find her place and purpose in the world?
3. Have you ever felt left out? What were the circumstances? Was anyone to blame?
4. How would you respond if the "candle plan" were imposed on you? If you were not Christian, how would it feel? Would you comply?
5. Do you have any neighbors who seem isolated? What steps can be taken to include them in the life of your neighborhood?
6. Why did Johnny's aching hands and knees stop bothering her? Will the problem recur?
7. If your home burned and everything was lost, what one item would you miss most?
8. Under what circumstances do you think Johnny will next get together with any of her neighbors? Where is the presence of God in this story?

A Place *for* Herod

Isaiah 7:10–16, Matthew 1:18–25

—

Ask a sign of . . . God; let it be deep as Sheol or high as heaven.

⤳ Isaiah 7:11

All this took place to fulfill what had been spoken by God through the prophet: "Look, the virgin shall conceive and bear a son, and they shall name him Emmanuel," which means, "God is with us."

⤳ Matthew 1:22–23

Sam was a very sad and frightened little girl. She was having a hard time concentrating on much of anything lately. She came home from school and holed up in her room day after day reading books and feeling sorry for herself. It was bad enough that her mother had remarried last year. And it was bad enough that they had left their old neighborhood and school and all of her good friends, including her best friend, Kimmy. And it was bad enough that Kimmy now had a new best friend, Alisha. And it was bad enough that she and her mother had moved out of their nice, cozy apartment for two into the new husband's big, ugly house. But now, her mother was about to have a baby! Samantha Jane McIntire wondered if anything else could possibly go wrong with her life. She was only twelve years old, and she felt utterly uncomfortable with everything—her home, her school, and, most dramatically, her family.

Sam questioned whether or not she actually had a family anymore. Her father did not seem to want to have anything to do with her—her real father, that is. He lived somewhere in Louisiana and never called or wrote or anything. Her new father (whom she knew she would never call anything but "Henry") offered what Sam considered to be superficial attempts at warmth. However, he meant nothing to her. Furthermore, Sam was determined that Henry would never be anything to her but some man her mother happened to marry.

Sam's mother was worried about her, and Sam knew it. But she did not know how to help her mother with this problem. She was not about to pretend that everything was hunky-dory when it was not. A baby! Sam loathed babies. In fact, her brief baby-sitting career had lasted for two hours one evening last summer, after which she swore she would never sink so low again. This baby, Sam knew, would take away what little time she had left with her mother in an average day. She hated that baby, and every time she looked at her swollen mother—now a few weeks from delivery—she was reminded of the horror of it all.

The arrival of Christmas was even more imminent. It was now seven days away, and Sam could not think of anything she wanted. Her mother kept asking for suggestions. Sam knew that if she handed her mother a list of the things she really wanted, it would only hurt her. She was very angry at her mother, but she had no desire to hurt her. The five things she really wanted were:

1. To move back to their old neighborhood.
2. To be in her old school with her own friends.

3. To have her mother decide that she did not really want to be married to Henry after all.
4. To make the stupid baby go away.
5. To have something from her real father for Christmas.

When they first moved into Henry's house, they also started attending Henry's church. Sam liked the music but thought the rest of it was pretty dumb. Some lady from the church had talked Sam into being in the Christmas pageant. Sam wished she had said "Thanks but no thanks," because the entire affair had turned into one big, humiliating disaster. This disaster could have been averted except for the fact that Sam hated pretending. She simply would not do it. She would not pretend that she was some desperately lonely new kid in the neighborhood who needed something to do. And she would not pretend that the Christmas story mattered to her one bit. After what happened on the first day of rehearsal, Sam decided, however, that sometimes a little pretending is the lesser of two evils.

What happened is this: All of the kids who came to the rehearsal (there were about twenty-five) drew a number out of a red and green wicker basket to see who got which part in the pageant. If you drew number 1, for instance, and you were a girl, you were supposed to want to be Mary, and you got the part. Naturally Sam picked number 1 out of the basket. Of all the luck! The pageant director said with great pride, "I guess this means our new Mary is Samantha McIntire. I think she will make a wonderful Mary!" Disappointed stares and grunts turned into great sighs of surprise and relief when Sam said that she did not, in fact, want to be Mary. She could tell that the other kids thought she must be crazy, and she did not care at all—at least she tried not to care. Anyway, Sam could not imagine being Mary, all puffed up like her mother. It was a nauseating notion.

"Who would you like to be, then?" the curious director inquired of her with a look of amazement.

"Herod," came the reply.

There was a moment of strained silence before the director said, in a kindly voice, "But we don't have a Herod in the Christmas pageant."

"Well, Herod is the only character I want to be in this thing."

The director took Sam aside and whispered, "Let me give it some thought."

The pageant lottery continued until every child had a part even if it meant donning sheep ears or angel wings. Samantha was thoroughly embarrassed. She knew her face had turned bright red during the incident, and she wished for all the world that she had never let this woman talk her into participating. The whole embarrassing affair played over and over again in her head, like a bad commercial that comes up at every break in the programming. Sam wondered how she could have handled it all differently. "I could have been a sheep," she said to herself as she sat on her bed on a sorry Friday afternoon shredding a purple ribbon into thin strips.

What Samantha had hoped after that dreadfully unlucky day was that Mrs. Houlton, the director, would call her back and say, "Since there is no room for Herod in the pageant, we would love for you to be a sheep." Instead, Mrs. Houlton conspired with the pastor to write Herod into the pageant script just so that Samantha could have what she wanted. So she was Herod, and she planned to make the best of it. She had only two lines, which were glorified versions of "What's the deal?" (asked of the wise guys) and "Go get'm!" (ordered to legions of armed soldiers who, the audience was supposed to imagine, were standing just outside the sanctuary to one side). She got to wear a golden crown and a blood-red robe, and she knew that she was pretty good at projecting her angry lines. She was torn between anticipation of her wicked role and really wanting the whole thing to be over. By tomorrow afternoon, it would be. "Tomorrow afternoon," she thought. "One more event I am *not* looking forward to," she said out loud to no one, even as she, in her own way, anticipated her remarkable performance.

*

Fourth Sunday, Year A

Sam envisioned a sanctuary full of eager pageant watchers admiring her highly convincing Herod. She pictured herself stealing the show away from meek little Mary and the laughably plastic baby. As she stood up to take an imaginary bow, letting the shredded pile of purple ribbon fall to the floor, she heard her mother yelling from downstairs. "Sammy! Sammy, get down here! You've got to call Henry." She ran downstairs to the kitchen where her mother was on her knees, bent over in pain. The floor was all wet. It was a scary sight. "Call Henry," her mother repeated when Sammy entered the kitchen. "He's at work. The number is right next to the phone."

"What's the matter, Mom?" Sam asked, trying to stay calm.

"Nothing's the matter, Sam. I think this baby has decided to arrive a little early, that's all."

Her mother seemed to be having trouble breathing. She looked, to Sam, as if she were dying.

"Are you sure, Mom?"

"Quite sure. Please call him. Do it now!" her mother ordered between gasps for air.

Sam raced to the phone and dialed the number with a shaky index finger. Henry's snooty secretary answered the phone, informing Sam that he was in an important meeting away from the office and could not be reached. This infuriated Sam, who told the secretary in no uncertain terms that she had better find him because his wife was about to have a baby. Sam did not even consult with her mother. She dialed 911 and demanded an ambulance. Her mother's face was all screwed up, her eyes were shut tight, and all Samantha could think was that if this was what it took to have a baby, she was never going to have one.

The ambulance arrived after a few minutes, during which Samantha stood in a panicked stupor over her mother, offering ineffective reassurances to her. "It's gonna be all right, Mom," she said, "I'll get you to the hospital." The driver of the ambulance told Sam she could come along, but she would have to stay in the front seat with a seat belt on. A scruffy-looking EMT, whom Sam thought rather good-looking, stayed in the back with her mother. Through a little window, Sam could see that her mother was getting an IV. Sam wondered if this was normal, but she was afraid to ask the driver. She wanted him to keep his eyes on the road and his mind focused on getting to the hospital.

The ride seemed interminably long, and she could hear her mother moaning wretchedly from the stretcher in the back. Sam thought she was acting quite cool and collected, but the driver must have noticed her anxiety, because, at some point, he said to her, "This is all perfectly normal, kid. Your mom will be fine." If this was all perfectly normal, thought Sam, childbearing is a cruel and terrible undertaking. It occurred to Sam that this was all Henry's fault, and she reminded herself never to get married.

When they arrived at the hospital, Sam's mother was hurriedly wheeled away, and Sam was ushered to a waiting room full of strangers in various states of distress. Empty seats were available, but Sam could not sit still. She bounced around the room, examining every poster, every painting, every sign. There was a small tabletop Christmas tree nestled in a corner of the room. It was covered with silver tinsel and little white paper cranes. A stack of square white paper sat on the end table beneath the tree along with detailed step-by-step instructions for making the cranes. Sam made three attempts but kept getting stuck on the fifth step. She stuffed her unfinished cranes into the back pocket of her jeans and hoped no one had been watching her.

She walked across the room and stared into two vending machines, wishing she had some change with her. She had not thought to bring anything with her. It had all happened so quickly. When Henry arrived in the waiting room, Sam was surprisingly glad to see his face. She offered him as much information as a twelve-year-old can. Then Henry told her that he was going to go find her mother. Without Sam's having to ask, Henry fished four single dollar bills and a pile of change out of his pocket and told her to get herself something to eat. He also told her that he would come back as soon as he had any information. Then he disappeared.

Sam thought that under the circumstances, she should not be hungry, but she was. She bought a bag of cheese curls and a can of soda. Having consumed these, she proceeded to the candy machine and chose a gooey chocolate delight. She had more than two dollars left but had reached her junk food limit. Finally, she sat down and flipped through a fashion magazine strewn among others on a low table. She figured that Henry had probably forgotten his promise to come back. Eventually, however, he did return. And when he did, he had a strikingly goofy look on his face. Henry said, "Well, I missed the birth, but everybody's fine, Sammy. Your mother is doing great, and you have a brand-new baby sister."

"What's its name?" she asked, trying to sound disinterested.

"We don't know yet. Maybe you have some ideas."

"Nah."

"Well, would you like to see her?"

"I guess so."

Henry led Samantha to a room on the second floor where her mother was resting in a stainless steel–sided bed. Next to her, in a clear plastic bassinet, was a tiny bundle wrapped in white blankets with a funny pink cotton stretch cap on its little head. Samantha wanted to stay away from it but was drawn by its squeaky little noises. Her mother said, "This is your sister. You want to hold her?" Samantha declined the invitation, suggesting that she would not know how. Over her protests, Henry picked up the small bundle and placed it in Samantha's arms. The baby was warm and seemed to snuggle right up into Samantha. She had squinty little eyes and a tiny rosebud of a mouth and a most perfect button nose.

What happened to Samantha in that holy moment is what has happened from the beginning of creation to mothers and fathers and siblings and grandparents and all flesh and blood whose hearts have

Fourth Sunday, Year A

melted uncontrollably in the presence of a lowly infant. Audible
sounds of awe rose from the center of Samantha's being. Herod fled.

Samantha's life did not suddenly turn into a journey of joy and
celebration that day. But she did begin to turn an important corner.
She gained a first layer of understanding Emmanuel, a first glimpse
of the irony and power and love of a God who arrives in the form of
an infant. She forgave her mother the treason of having another
child and allowed a tiny seed of gratitude for family to sprout in her
soul. And in the pageant she offered a very unconvincing Herod.

Questions for Reflection and Discussion

1. What was the most difficult aspect of Sam's life? Why is she so
   sad? Why is she frightened?
2. Why does Sam dislike Henry so much? Would she dislike any
   father figure at this point in her life? Do you have any suggestions for Henry?
3. Why does Sam hate pretending? When was the last time you
   pretended to be someone you were not or to feel something you
   did not? Is pretending ever necessary?
4. Create a Christmas list for Sam. Include on this list what you
   think Sam really wants.
5. Was Samantha's announcement that she wanted to be Herod an
   act of courage or simply an outpouring of anger?
6. Are there steps that Mrs. Houlton could have taken to include
   Sam without adding the part of Herod? Did she make a wise
   decision? Why or why not?
7. What happened when Sam held the baby? Have you had an
   experience like this?
8. Did Sam experience Emmanuel? If so, how?

Yards *of* Purple

Isaiah 64:1–9, Mark 13:24–37

—

O that you would tear open the heavens and come down, so that the mountains would quake at your presence.

        ⬧ Isaiah 64:1

From the fig tree learn its lesson: as soon as its branch becomes tender and puts forth its leaves, you know that summer is near. So also, when you see these things taking place, you know that it is near, at the very gates.

        ⬧ Mark 13:28–29

*L*ydia had been sitting at her uncooperative sewing machine for an eternity when the mail came. It was Saturday morning, about ten o'clock, and the mail always came a little bit earlier on Saturdays, in order, she supposed, that the letter carrier could start the already abbreviated weekend as soon as possible. Lydia usually slept in on Saturdays, but it was exactly four weeks until Christmas, and she was determined to take all of that fabric she had just bought and turn it into four stunning dresses for her four mostly cute but sometimes

34

obnoxious nieces. Lydia's two sisters each had two daughters, and, although she was the eldest, Lydia was not even married. She was the only one still carrying the Nelson name. When she looked at her rambunctious nieces, sometimes she was very happy about that fact, but at other times, she had to admit, she longed for a family of her own. Perhaps the time would come. "Hear that, God?" She willed her thoughts heavenward.

There she sat, by herself, for the most part enjoying her solitude and the gentle voices of easy-listening music on her stereo, staring at yards upon yards of purple fabric. Each one of her nieces was in a purple phase. Actually, come to think of it, these four were ladies of perpetual purple. She could not think of a time when there had been an alternate favorite color in any of their lives. While Lydia thought reds and blues were far more becoming on these little girls, she figured she had better go purple. After all, these nieces of hers would already be disappointed. She knew that. They counted on their Aunt Lydia for beautiful store-bought gifts, always selected from the Christmas lists they themselves had generated—lists that were already hanging on the side of Lydia's refrigerator. They counted on their Aunt Lydia to be generous.

Well, this year would be different. It was not that she wanted to abandon her generosity; it was just that she did not want to be so predictable. She was seeking a more personalized form of generosity. And she was, quite frankly, tired of feeling a little taken for granted. She was tired of the mall. She was tired of the post-Thanksgiving shopping frenzy. She was tired of a lot of things. Lydia wanted this Christmas to be different. This year, she wanted to put more care into her gift-giving, more of herself into her preparations. She thought she might even go to church for a change. She wanted to anticipate more than a Christmas morning free-for-all, something greater but harder to define, something like the rebirth of her soul. Still, she questioned whether or not she had done the right thing, spending her Christmas club money on fabric and patterns when she had not sewn anything in at least five years. Could she even finish these dresses in the free time she had left between now and Christmas?

She had sorted out the purples early this morning. The palest lavender with Swiss dots was for Anna, the youngest; the purple-on-purple cabbage-rose print (quite a find) was for Cheryl, the eldest niece; and the purple calicos were for Ellie and Fiona, the two seven-year-old cousins who were fast friends and fierce competitors. Lydia selected what had looked like easy patterns, which she figured she would dress up with white piping and lace. She cut out the first dress, Anna's, and had been at it since seven o'clock. She sat there, repinning the left sleeve for the third time, having changed broken needles twice, when she saw the mail carrier leave a bundle in the box. She thought she should really finish the sleeves and the zipper before allowing herself to be distracted. After all, she had her work cut out for her. Feeling suddenly overwhelmed by the enormity of the task, however, she decided to fetch the mail. "One distraction, that's all," she mused. "I'll just sort through the mail and then get back to stitching."

In the mailbox, she found a fat package full of coupons, several local store flyers pushing various Christmas deals, yet another Molly Herndon catalog, a telephone bill, a postcard from the Red Cross announcing the next blood drive, and a hand-addressed envelope from Mary Morgens, Lydia's aunt from Michigan. Lydia had not heard from her Aunt Mary in . . . well, it had to be several years. She opened the envelope with eager anticipation and found a short note along with a check for two hundred dollars. Aunt Mary indicated that all was well and told her to do something wonderful with the money. Lydia thought that this must be a sign. This was God's way of saying, "Give yourself a break. Go to the mall. Buy those nieces of yours something they will really like, and let the fabric take a new, less-tortuous path." Before she could even permit herself time to think about the matter further, Lydia grabbed her purse, snatched the Christmas lists, locked the door, and set out for the mall. It was a lovely day, and she lived only a twenty-minute walk away. The bank was right in the mall. She could cash the check there, buy four spectacular gifts, have them wrapped by the Girl Scouts right there, and be done with it.

Her walk to the mall was energetic, determined. The great weight of seemingly endless stitching had been lifted from her frustrated fingers. Heading straight for the bank and exchanging Aunt Mary's check for four crisp new fifty-dollar bills, she stuffed her newfound financial freedom into her pocket and strode toward PlayWorld. Heading straight for the doll section, she pulled out one of the last sets of "Fuss and Giggle" triplets from the shelf and checked off little Anna from her mental list of niecely burdens. Noticing that there was, for the moment, no line at the cash register in this very busy place, she ran for it, plopping the triplets on the counter. "That'll be $26.49," said a very young clerk with gravity-defying bangs. Lydia reached deep into her pocket and . . . it was empty. Her heart sank like a lump of clay. She checked the other pocket. Empty. Her jeans pockets. Empty. "Oh no," she said to the clerk in frantically hushed tones, "the money's gone."

Retracing her steps through the brimming mall, she found nothing. At a brisk pace, she located a guard and was directed to the mall security office, where she reported the loss and was told by her stony listener, "It's as good as gone, lady, but if by some miracle we find it, we'll give you a call." The first half of Lydia's walk home was laborious. She felt just plain stupid. Had someone picked her pocket? Had the money simply fallen out? In either case, why had she so casually stuffed it into her pocket? Why had she not taken the time to put it away in the purse that hung limply from her shoulder? Her attitude shifted, however, as she drew closer to home. She thought, maybe this is the real sign. Perhaps this whole morning had been a symbol that she, Lydia "D. for Dumb" Nelson, had allowed herself to be blown about like a leaf in the wind in many ways and certainly by the pressures of impending Christmas. She needed to regroup, regain her composure, reestablish the kind of preparation for which she had originally hoped. All was not lost. This year could be different.

Dennis Jones also lived near the mall. As he walked toward this great behemoth of goods and services, he reviewed the terrible year which had led to this desperate time. His young wife, Marie, had died almost exactly a year ago after a relentless illness. His son, Alex, now seventeen, and daughter, Elizabeth, fifteen, seemed endlessly sad, but they were coping. There were some good days, but every day held some inescapable reminder of the emptiness they all felt. Then three months ago, Dennis was suddenly "let go." He lost his job and had not been able to find another. Here it was four weeks before Christmas, and he had no money. His visit to the mall was intended to be another search for "Help Wanted" signs. Surely someone in the mall would need extra Christmas help. Surely someone would be as eager for help as he was for work.

He wanted so much to be able to buy Elizabeth a dress. She had been invited to the junior Christmas prom but did not have a proper dress, and stoically told her father that she really was not all that interested in a silly dance anyway. But he knew better. His son, Alex, needed new basketball shoes. Dennis really wanted to buy him the shoes for Christmas. Not the ridiculously expensive "in your face" basketball shoes—just a decent pair that would carry him through the season. But Dennis was broke. He was broker than broke. His friends at church had been great, helping with food and rent, but he could not possibly ask them for money for a party dress and basket-ball shoes. Dennis believed that God works for those who wait, but waiting, he had discovered, was difficult and scary.

When he entered Hope Bridge Mall, he thought he had never seen so many people in one place before. "The race is on," he reasoned, his response to the crowd mingled with both excitement and despair. Nearing the bank, he stopped and recalled that only two years ago he had had a fair-sized account there. Shaking his head he noticed what looked like money in one corner of the tiled mall floor. Stooping down, he picked up four crisp new fifty-dollar bills. "Is this a sign," he wondered, "a sign that all is not lost? Have the heavens been torn open, and has God's grace tumbled into this little corner of Hope Bridge Mall?"

Dennis looked around and tucked the fortuitous bills into his empty wallet. He headed for Ruby's Elegant Dress Shop, where he spied in the display window a magnificent three-quarter-length holly-berry red dress with princess sleeves, and immediately pictured his daughter dancing at the Christmas prom. Stepping inside the exclusive shop, a shop in which his wife had drooled over many a fashion statement, he checked the price tag on the red dress: $129.99. $129.99! Did they think they were really fooling anybody with that 99-cent trickery? Well, he had $130 with him now, and he could well imagine the delight in Elizabeth's eyes when he presented this beautiful gift to her.

But . . . he knew this was not his money after all. Clearly someone had lost this money, perhaps someone in more desperate straits than he. The guilt he had felt in the instant he picked up the enticing money had caught up with him. Torn and empty-handed, he left Ruby's. Looking for a mall map, Dennis saw that a security office was tucked in a small space off by itself, and he set out reluctantly, but in good conscience, to turn in the screaming money.

Having found the office, Dennis also found an unexpectedly familiar face. The fellow sitting behind the desk was a high-school classmate—not someone he knew well, but certainly someone he remembered by name: Bill Geisler. Bill was something of a math whiz, and Dennis was a little surprised to find him in the garb of a mall security guard. "Bill," he said, "my name is Dennis. Dennis Jones. We went to school together, I think."

"Dennis, yes," replied the visibly brightening security guard, "Dennis. I remember. Go Golden Geese! How the heck are you, Dennis?"

First Sunday, Year B

Dennis and Bill sat there for almost an hour, swapping stories, each sharing what the last twenty-five years had held. Upon discovering that Dennis was out of work, Bill mentioned a job that had just opened up and said he would be happy to introduce Dennis to the right people. Dennis felt some hope in these words because he had come to understand that in the long unemployment line, it is not *what* you know but *who* you know. Eventually, Dennis mustered the moral courage to pull out the four fifty-dollar bills and tell his friend where and how he had found them.

"Whoa," responded Bill, "most people would have that money spent already!" Dennis laughed and answered honestly that he had considered spending it. With a smile on his face, he told Bill about Elizabeth's dress and Alex's shoes.

"Well, sit here a minute, Dennis, and I'll give this woman a call. I know she'll be as amazed as I am that the money has turned up." Bill went into a back room, where the phone sat on a messy desk. He reached Lydia Nelson on the third ring.

Lydia had made significant progress. It was only 3:30 in the afternoon and, except for the hem, she was finished with Anna's dress, had already cut out Ellie's and Fiona's, and was well under way with Ellie's. On her transforming walk home from the mall, Lydia's enthusiasm for her handmade presents had grown and filled her with newfound purpose and vigor.

"God works in mysterious ways," she thought as the stitches flew. She felt strangely blessed at having lost that money. She had come very close to "predictable" again this year and had been saved by an empty pocket. Why, she felt downright thankful and hoped with all her heart that whoever found that money had put it to better use than she would have. "Fuss and Giggle triplets!" she said out loud and laughed at the ridiculousness of it all. How could they possibly compare with the beautiful dress that now hung sweetly on a hanger on the doorknob next to her?

When the phone rang, Lydia had to force herself to get up from the now cooperative sewing machine. "The money has been found?" she asked in disbelief. "Well, how? Where? Who found it?" Bill quickly told her the touching story of the poor unemployed fellow who had nearly spent it on a dress for his daughter and shoes for his son but was honest and concerned enough to turn it in.

"Who is he?" she asked.

"He . . . he's sitting in the next room," said Bill. "Would you like to thank him yourself? I'll put him on the phone."

"No!" she exclaimed to the surprised security guard. Then she continued, "Tell him to keep it. Tell him to buy the dress and the shoes. Tell him how grateful I am to him, and tell him I no longer need that money."

"Are you sure, ma'am?" asked Bill.

Lydia thought of Aunt Mary's words: "Do something wonderful with it."

"I've never been more sure of anything in my life," she answered, feeling so thankful to have been reshaped by the divine Potter, and heading back to her yards of purple.

Questions for Reflection and Discussion

1. Why did the girls count on Aunt Lydia to be generous? Was she? How so? Have you ever been generous only to end up feeling taken for granted?

2. Why was Lydia tired of so many things? Are you tired of anything?

3. When Lydia first received the two hundred dollars in the mail, she thought it must be a sign. Then she thought that losing the money could be a sign. Dennis thought that finding the money was a sign. Were any of these divine signs? How can you tell a true sign?

4. Why did Dennis return the money? Would you?

5. Lydia felt saved by an empty pocket. Has this ever happened to you? Could it?

6. Lydia sensed that she had been reshaped by the divine Potter. How so? Will it last?

7. Do you imagine Lydia will ever meet Dennis? Under what circumstances?

8. Who experienced the grace of God more deeply, Lydia or Dennis?

Prepare Ye *the* Way

Isaiah 40:1–11, Mark 1:1–8

—

Every valley shall be lifted up, and every mountain and hill be made low; the uneven ground shall become level, and the rough places a plain. Then the glory of God shall be revealed, and all people shall see it together, for the mouth of God has spoken.

⤳ Isaiah 40:4–5

I have baptized you with water; but he will baptize you with the Holy Spirit.

⤳ Mark 1:8

Eric's mother was making him go to church. He did not want to go, and he intended, therefore, to make it perfectly clear that this was not his choice, that he was going against his will. Eric was fourteen, and he was quite certain that no other fourteen-year-old he knew would be in church, that none of his friends had parents who made them go to church. "Church is boring," he complained to his mother. When this produced no reaction, he continued, "The music is boring. The minister is boring. Only old people go to church," he

43

said, with the emphasis on "old" so that his mother would know exactly where he placed her on the age scale. "You might be surprised," she answered him cheerfully. "Try to go with an open mind," Eric's father interjected, winking at him. Eric grunted.

"Try to go with an open mind," he murmured to himself and winked cynically into his disheveled closet. He looked for something fitting to wear and quickly dismissed the two seldom-worn dress shirts hanging there in favor of a wrinkled sweatshirt with the word "Fearless" boldly printed on the back. This treasured article of clothing was conveniently crumpled on the floor of the closet. Opening the bottom drawer of his dresser, he shoved his good pants out of the way, uncovering a pair of jeans with a big hole in the right knee.

Rebelliously dressed, Eric declared himself "ready for church" before his parents, who sat at the kitchen table sipping steaming cups of café latte. He expected a small war. He expected, at the very least, to be sent back up to his room in order to find something more appropriate. After a momentary exchange of knowing nods between his parents, however, his father said, "Well, you might as well be comfortable." "I don't think God cares what you wear," his mother added.

A somewhat confused Eric sneaked back upstairs and changed into a decent pair of khakis, a button-down shirt, and a navy silk tie that was reserved for school concerts and other august occasions. His parents pretended not to notice the change, but Eric observed his father wink knowingly at his mother. What's with the wink? Eric winced with a certain disdain for his painfully "uncool" parents.

The drive to church was uneventful. His mother tried to engage him in light conversation, but, as an effective part of his ongoing protest, Eric delivered short monotone answers to her queries.

"It's a beautiful day, don't you think, Eric?"

"It's OK."

"When was the last time we went to church?"

"Last Christmas."

"I think it was actually two years ago, on Christmas Eve," his father amended.

"Do you think that same minister is still there?"

"Probably."

"I think Wendy Larkin goes to this church."

"Doubt it," Eric answered, but privately he grew slightly more enthusiastic about the whole operation and was glad he had not worn the jeans with the hole in the knee after all. Wendy Larkin and Eric had been in the same classes since the second grade and he had a long-standing crush on her, which was, apparently, no secret to his mother. How do mothers know these things? he wondered.

As they pulled into the parking lot, Eric could see that the lot was filling quickly. There seemed to be children everywhere heading for the main doors of the building. With a note of sarcasm gently aimed at her glum son, his mother said, "Look at all these old people." "There's some," Eric quickly retorted, pointing to three elegant silver-haired ladies who were just emerging from a big car parked in a "handicap" spot. "They look dangerous," said his mother. "I think you are surrounded," said his father.

Eric was surprised at how bright the church was. He remembered it being a shadowy place, but then again, it had been a while. Church was, at worst, a biyearly phenomenon. His understanding of "church" was built largely of images gleaned from television. Some of the words that described his media picture of church were "spooky," "guilty," "severe," and "gloomy." Maybe he had never been to church in the morning before—that was probably it. Someone greeted them at the door saying, "Welcome! Glad to see you here this morning." This welcome person was no one Eric knew. He rolled his eyeballs dramatically to let the greeter know that he was here under duress.

The sanctuary was nearly filled, and, to make matters worse, Eric and his parents had to sit in the second row, right up front. He slunk into his seat, let his head fall onto his chest, and folded his arms over

his stomach as if to say, "Just try to get through to me. Just try it."
Out of the corner of his eye, he noticed Danny DiNotti and slunk
even further into his self-imposed cocoon. "Danny de Nut," the kids
at school called him, and sometimes "Danny de Nothing." Danny
was probably the least popular kid in the eighth grade. He was a new
kid in the school who had moved here from California, "where all
the nuts come from," his friend Tyler had said. Nobody talked to
him. Who would?

There was something wrong with Danny's foot, and he walked
funny and could not do much of anything in gym class. Eric remembered someone telling him that Danny had been born with a club
foot—whatever that is—and his foot had to be completely recon-
structed, but it would never be a normal foot. Eric was sure that
whatever a club foot was, it must be terrible, and he was glad he was
not born with one. He felt sorry for Danny and all, but he was not
about to destroy his social life by being nice to him. Stealthily, Eric
glanced over at Danny again and thanked God that Danny had not
yet noticed him sitting there.

While the organ played something that Eric recognized as suitably
tiresome for church, he imagined saying "Told you so" to his mother.
He felt vindicated. Church is boring! His mind wandered back to
Danny de Nothing, and Eric hoped he could make it out of church
without having to say anything to him. Once, back in September,
Danny had sat down at the same lunch table as Eric and had offered
him one of his snack cakes. Eric had accepted the treat, and it was a
full two weeks before his friends stopped ridiculing him for befriend-
ing Danny de Nut. Eric was determined never to let that happen
again.

The music stopped, and an old woman who reminded Eric of his
fifth-grade teacher began to speak. Eric turned to his father and
silently mouthed the word "boring." His father whispered in his
unreceptive ear, "Your vocabulary needs some fresh material." Eric
glared out the window and noticed a small flock of tiny birds resting

on the branches of a nearly bare tree. They looked cold, pitiable, and they appeared to be looking directly at him. It was weird. His father nudged him as everyone stood to sing the opening hymn. He did not know the hymn but pretended to sing, being sure to keep his face hidden in the hymnal just in case Danny looked over his way. Everyone sat down again, and the woman introduced something called the prayer of confession. "What do I have to confess?" Eric whispered to his father while staring at the prayer in the bulletin. "You'll think of something," his father whispered back. Eric read the prayer along with everyone else in the room.

> Dear God, we hear the words "Prepare the way of God," but we do not know how to prepare. We hear you cry, "Make the rough places smooth," but we do not know how to do this. Forgive the obstacles and rough places we place in your path and in the paths of our neighbors. Forgive our handi-capped hearts. Forgive the hurt we bring into one another's lives, and teach us to prepare for the birth of the Christ child into our hearts again this season. Amen.

"Forgive our handicapped hearts." The words hit him like a sur-prise math test. They dug themselves into his young conscience, pre-senting Eric with one of those rare and holy moments of revealed truth. Eric, quite suddenly and very unexpectedly, felt sorry—deeply sorry—for the hurt he had caused Danny. For the first time, it dawned on him how thoroughly awful and lonely Danny must feel. Eric imagined himself with a club heart, a heart unable to beat prop-erly or to love properly, even as Danny's foot made it impossible for him to walk like everyone else.

Eric's eyes were drawn to the window again, where he watched the small birds fly away. In his own fledgling soul, he had experienced the judgment of God. He prayed silently, "Forgive my handicapped heart. Forgive the hurt I have brought into Danny's life." It was not an earthshaking "road to Damascus" change, but it was significant. Most mountains are made low and most valleys filled not in an instant but over a period of time.

"Peace be with you," said the woman up front, and suddenly people were getting up and offering words of peace to one another. Eric sat startled, listening to the words reverberate around the room. "Peace be with you. Peace be with you. Peace be with you." He was surrounded. Staring into his bulletin, Eric realized that someone was standing in front of him. He looked up, and there was Danny meekly saying, "The peace of Christ be with you." "Thanks. . . .Uh, you too," replied Eric. The words felt awkward, yet somehow right. This wounded boy, who had every right to hate Eric, had offered him peace.

The sermon followed the same theme, "Prepare Ye the Way of God." Eric yawned his way through the part about John the Baptist being a member of a strict Jewish sect. This part he would later describe to his father, with an inherited wink and the help of his desk thesaurus, as "dull, dreary, tedious, and uninteresting." He did, however, listen surprisingly closely to the part about inner preparations. He had always thought of Christmas preparations as being outer things—garlands and wreaths and ornaments and such. The preparation the minister was talking about was different. It had to do with being cleansed on the inside, turning and walking in a new direction. It had to do with being forgiven. He found himself believing that it was possible for the crooked within himself to be made straight, and the rough ways smooth, and his own handicapped heart strengthened and mended. And if a Christ child was to be born into human hearts, he imagined that he could probably make room in his own. Probably.

He honestly did not know what to make of Holy Communion except that it kept bringing to his mind the snack-cake episode. Then, at the end of the service, after another hymn which Eric did not recognize in the least, the minister stood in the back and said,

"Prepare the way! Make straight in the desert a highway for our God! Every valley shall be lifted up and every mountain and hill be made low; the uneven ground shall become level, and the rough places a plain. Then the glory of God shall be revealed." Then he added, "May the God of hope fill you with all joy and peace in believing, so that you may abound in hope by the power of the Holy Spirit."

On their way home, Eric's mother said, "I guess I was wrong about Wendy Larkin. I didn't see her there." "Yeah," replied Eric, who stared out of the car window pensively. "Who was that funny kid who came over to you during the service?" "A friend," answered Eric. And they went home to continue their preparations.

Questions for Reflection and Discussion

1. Why did Eric not want to go to church? Why are so many young people uninterested in the church?
2. Why did Eric put on nicer clothes? Do you think there are people who stay away from church because they fear their clothing will be judged? Can anything be done about this?
3. Why did Eric think of the church as a shadowy place?
4. How did Eric feel when he first noticed Danny sitting near him? Have you ever intentionally avoided someone? What were your reasons?
5. Why did Eric think the birds were looking at him? What triggers a conscience?
6. Eric began to put himself in Danny's shoes. Where does empathy begin? How can empathy be taught?
7. What do you think will happen the next time Eric sees Danny?
8. Was Eric touched by the Holy Spirit? How can you tell?

Second Sunday, Year B

Liberty to *the* Captives

Isaiah 61:1–4, 8–11, John 1:6–8, 19–28

—

The spirit of the Sovereign God is upon me, because God has anointed me; God has sent me to bring good news to the oppressed, to bind up the brokenhearted, to proclaim liberty to the captives, and release to the prisoners.

Isaiah 61:1

The true light, which enlightens everyone, was coming into the world.

John 1:9

There were twelve of us crammed into the quaint little elevator when it got stuck—stuck right between the second and third floors of the Garland Street Nursing Home. The sign in the elevator, which we all read thoroughly (long after our cozy stay in the elevator began), indicated a maximum weight of one thousand pounds. In my usual minimalist math fashion, I swiftly calculated that the elevator could hold ten persons, each weighing one hundred pounds. Surveying our immobilized group with no less mental acuity, I ascertained that we had brought with us into the elevator far more heft than that. It seemed like good fun at the time. We all fit! We simply (emphasis on the simple) assumed that if we fit into the elevator, we would be fine. I laughed as my husband leaned into the compressed assembly, feeling the doors slide closed against his prominent posterior. The group continued to giggle for one and a half floors worth of "up."

David and Bubba, both imposingly athletic college guys, probably brought five hundred pounds into the elevator all by themselves. Squished in with them were Everett and Marian Farnham, a youngish couple, both tall (and thankfully slim); their two spindly offspring, Aaron and Emily; Frank Nash, a jolly, stoop-shouldered retired fellow for whom this event had become an important yearly ritual; my husband, Hank, who is built like a linebacker (which, as you will discover, came in quite handy in the end); a medium-sized single mom named Gloria with her doe-eyed little girl, Chelsea; Reverend Turner, who, like so many ministers, carries a proud paunch studiously developed through the consumption of countless home-made cookies and brownies offered to him by grateful and well-meaning parishioners; and me (and you can bet I'm not about to give you any indication of my own sorry girth). My extremely rough estimate of the weight in the elevator was fifteen hundred pounds. In any event, it was enough to bring the elevator to a grinding halt before it could reach its destination, the third floor.

Waiting for us up on the third floor was Hildy Olsen, a ninety-two-year-old charter member of the church, who was having a hard time getting around in recent days and who eagerly awaited our piti-ful rendition of "Silent Night," while we were stuck, unbeknownst to her, in the elevator. You see, every year, on the Sunday before Christmas Eve, the church we all happened to attend encouraged anyone who wished, to go Christmas caroling to various home-bound persons. Garland Street was our first stop. It was not, as you may have guessed, one of those fancy places where the genteel elderly rich spend their final years surrounded by lovely gilt-framed Impressionist prints, Oriental rugs, and fresh flowers. Rather, it was one of those state-assisted facilities that house those who cannot afford any-place else and whose families (if they have families) cannot or will not take them in. In Hildy's case, there was no immediate family. We were it.

The halls of Garland Street were hung with paint-by-number art-works rendered by the residents themselves. A dusty bowl of pink silk roses sat on a scratched table near the entrance. Cheap metallic Christmas tinsel had been strung throughout. I spotted three or four faded cardboard Santa faces posted at eye level, each one trying its best to offer cheer in a not-so-cheery place. Taped to the door of each resident's room was a paper angel. Each angel had the resident's first name written on it. The expressions on the angel faces differed according to the demeanor and artistic ability of the person who, through the magic of markers, summoned the face on to the paper.

Hildy was a relatively new resident of Garland Street and, while she did not especially like it, she understood that she did not have very many alternatives at her age and in her position. One of her chief complaints was that she had not made any friends there. Her lack of mobility was the problem. She was taking most of her meals in her room. Reverend Turner had brought a folding wheelchair to her and encouraged her to try it, but Hildy was steadfastly resistant to the idea. She wanted to be up on her own two feet and saw the wheelchair as a symbol that her independence was nearly gone. "If you used the wheelchair," he tried to convince her, "you could go down to the common room every day and play bingo with the others. They have a great time, you know." "Bingo!" She spat the word out as if it were dirt. He had proposed the wrong activity. His suggestion only enhanced her resolve to remain in her room until she could be up and around on her own. Reverend Turner, while a great believer in miracles, knew that dramatic improvement was unlikely.

Everett Farnham proved to be somewhat claustrophobic, and when he realized what had happened, he began pushing buttons frantically, hoping to evoke some sort of response from the very mechanisms that held us soundly imprisoned in the elevator. Needless to say, no such response was forthcoming. Everett's daughter, Emily, who was standing just beneath him, tugged at his coat sleeve, a bright silver Christmas bell jangling around her neck, until he finally looked down. She said, "There's a phone here, Daddy. Call somebody." Sure enough, just below the panel of buttons was a small stainless steel door with a picture of a phone imprinted on it. Reverend Turner, who was plastered to the wall on the opposite side of the elevator, suggested that he place the call, but everyone agreed it would be painfully difficult to maneuver him around to the phone corner of the elevator. He said he would pray instead, encouraged everyone else to do the same, and told Everett to pick up the phone and place the call. I watched Reverend Turner close his frightened eyes. The Farnhams followed suit, as did little Emily.

I had a hard time praying as I was busy being very grateful to whoever had first come up with the idea of putting emergency phones in elevators. Scanning the would-be choir, I noticed that little Chelsea's eyes were red, and she was anxiously sucking her upper lip into her mouth so that she looked like a little female version of Stan Laurel (of Laurel and Hardy). I was not the only one to notice, because within milliseconds of my spotting her imminent tears, Bubba further strained the sardine can by bending down to reassure her. "It's gonna be okay," he declared. "God'll get us outta here." Bubba continued to gently reassure Chelsea with softly spoken words of faith in God. No offense, God, I thought to myself, but I'm counting on whoever is at the other end of that phone.

Unfortunately, the person at the other end of the line, the emergency technician, was at a location three hours away. She said she would call for a mechanic, but, as it was a Sunday evening and so close to Christmas and all, it might be several hours. The words "several hours" were very upsetting to everyone (even though we did not all demonstrate it). They were extremely upsetting to Chelsea, who started to bawl rather loudly. Bubba, big hulk of a guy though he was (I think he was on the wrestling team), put his arm around Chelsea's shoulder and told her what an adventure it was and how we would all be laughing when it was over. His deep, calm voice seemed to soothe her, and her wail was lowered to a soft whimper. Chelsea's mother, Gloria, oddly silent while all of this was going on, just watched. She appeared to be thankful that someone else was handling the upset while she struggled to cope with her own active insecurities.

As the reality of our unexpected situation set in, people began to talk about what this delay meant. Bubba and David openly wondered how long they would be stuck, because they had a final exam for which to study. Squeezing in the Christmas caroling had already entailed pushing their schedules into a probable all-nighter. The Farnhams were concerned about the lateness of the hour because it was a school night, after all, and Aaron had a small case of the sniffles. The kids needed their sleep. Gloria looked down at Chelsea and nodded. Frank Nash, looking more chipper than ever with his Santa hat and Christmas holly tie, was the only one who did not seem to care. He was happy to say that he had no place to be and no schedule to keep. I think most of us were annoyed by that fact. The truth was that I did not have any pressing engagements, either. I was too embarrassed to admit that my primary frustration with the situation was that if we were stuck there for long, I would miss my favorite Sunday-night police drama.

I had never been stuck in an elevator before, and I could not think of a single acquaintance who had ever been through this loaded experience, either. I thought this was the ludicrous sort of drama that only happens on television. It was fiction of the sitcom variety:

You know, pregnant woman gets stuck in elevator with clueless copy-machine repairman, who miraculously delivers healthy baby to mother who is weeping tears of joy and gratitude. Plain-looking young man with little confidence gets stuck in elevator with voluptuous young woman who, eventually, brings out the best in him. Neighbors who cannot stand one another must spend five hours stuck in the elevator together and emerge as friends for life. You never hear anything about a motley church group getting stuck in an old nursing-home elevator. It would never sell.

Reverend Turner, trying to find the silver lining in this compressed December cloud, suggested that we put the time to good use by practicing Christmas carols. With some reluctance on my part, I joined the others in a clumsy rendition of "Come, Thou Long-Expected Jesus." The words "born to set thy people free" were not lost on us. To dispel our gloom, we sang "Joy to the World." Through our obvious dismay, we sang "God Rest Ye Merry, Gentlemen." The kids were eagerly teaching the adults "We three kings of Orient are, tried to smoke a rubber cigar. It was loaded. It exploded . . ." when suddenly the phone rang. Everett grabbed the receiver and listened to the operator. In silence, we watched his deadpan face and heard him say, "I see. Well, thank you." Our hearts sank as he explained to us that an elevator mechanic had been located, but it would be at least two hours before he would arrive to save us.

Through our moans of disappointment, we could hear some muffled yelling on the other side of the elevator. "Quiet!" Reverend Turner said. Through the top of the elevator door, we heard someone saying—quite distinctly, I might add—"How about 'Away in a Manger'?" Somebody on the third floor was listening! Perhaps the evening was not a bust after all. Since this is his favorite of the Christmas hymns, my husband, Hank, started us off. When we finished the words, asking God to "fit us for heaven to live with thee there," we heard immediate chants for "Rudolph," which we offered willingly. After that, a familiar voice called out, "Why don't you just pry open the door?" We had not thought of that. My husband, whose back was pressed up tight against the door, did not wait for any discussion of the matter. Deftly he rotated himself around, jammed his big hands into the door opening, and with effectively manly grunting, tore open the doors. We were free. There was no shortage of *Thank Gods* in that merry moment.

Through the opened doors, we saw that the third floor was only about two feet above us. A crowd of twenty or more nursing home residents were neatly clustered at the elevator door. In the middle of them sat Hildy in her borrowed wheelchair, beaming as she recognized us. "Well, you finally made it!" she exclaimed. "We're getting tired, you know." Hank said, "We would have sung 'Why Don't You Just Pry Open the Door?' but none of us knew all the words." To that, Hildy offered a contagious and gut-busting laugh.

One of the nurses at Garland Street, a lovely woman named Grace, had known that the church group was coming and was the first to figure out what had happened to the elevator. She was the one who finally convinced Hildy to get into the wheelchair and come listen to the singing. Hildy's neighbors joined her with enthusiasm. One of them wangled a plate of cookies out of the kitchen staff and they turned the stuck-elevator incident into a third-floor party the likes of which no one had seen before.

Hildy discovered a few new friends that night. And once we had boosted everyone out of the elevator, the rest of us did, too. Garland Street was our first and last stop that night. Reverend Turner, nibbling on a sugar cookie, proposed that the youth group visit the other homebound persons later in the week. Frank Nash said that he would gladly organize a midweek continuation of the caroling event for the youth group and for anyone else who wanted to go. David and Bubba postponed their studies a bit longer in order to swap stories with their elders. Little Chelsea carefully inspected a miniature Christmas tree that a sweet old lady named Doris brought over to show her. Gloria looked on in wonder. My glowing husband cheer-fully received the many compliments offered to him on his impressive strength. Everett and Marian gathered their young and readied themselves to leave. Before they left, however, at the suggestion of Grace, we ended the evening with a remarkably lovely "Silent night, holy night. All is calm, all is bright, round yon virgin mother and child. Holy infant, so tender and mild, sleep in heavenly peace. Sleep in heavenly peace."

I think we all learned something that night. I learned not to underestimate big, athletic types named Bubba. I learned that brute strength can be a good thing. I learned, once again, that God works in mysterious ways to comfort and to free. And I think that at the age of ninety-two, yielding to the wheelchair, Hildy learned that what appear to be shackles and chains can actually be the means to freedom, and what seems like freedom may be the very thing that holds us captive.

Questions for Reflection and Discussion

1. The days before Christmas can be especially difficult for those who live alone. Do you know of anyone in this situation? What can be done to create an extended family for this person?
2. Why did Hildy refuse to use the wheelchair? Can you think of a situation in which you stubbornly refused help or in which your help was stubbornly refused? Why was assistance refused?
3. Did Reverend Turner's praying help solve the problem in the elevator? Why or why not?
4. Bubba was tender and compassionate to little Chelsea. Why did this come as a surprise? In what ways do we underestimate or overestimate a person based on appearance?
5. People were frustrated in the stuck elevator for a variety of reasons. What were they? What would be most difficult for you if you were stuck in an elevator?

6. After the elevator incident, all the participants changed their plans a little. Suddenly, their schedules were not as important as seizing the moment. Why was that?

7. How was Hildy both comforted and freed that evening? Who else was comforted or freed?

8. How does God comfort us? How does God free us?

Unconditional Companionship

2 Samuel 7:1–11, Luke 1:26–38

—

Nathan said to the king, "Go, do all that you have in mind; for God is with you." . . . and I have been with you wherever you went.

⟿ 2 Samuel 7:3, 9a

Then Mary said, "Here am I, the servant of God; let it be with me according to your word."

⟿ Luke 1:38

It was already three o'clock on Saturday afternoon, and Luke had not even begun to think about tomorrow morning's sermon. He was generally more organized than this, but it had been a heavy week. Crisis calls: It was not unusual for people to unravel a bit under the weight of Christmas preparations. Hospital visits: A particularly nasty pneumonia was accompanying a bitter cold snap. Special seasonal events: The women's Christmas dinner, the annual nursing home Christmas cookie event, the preparation of food baskets for folks in the community who would not otherwise have much of a Christmas dinner, and a big ecumenical church choir concert that Luke helped to organize as a way of raising funds for a much-needed family shelter.

His office was a mess. Amid the chaos were the usual stacks of unopened junk mail, an assortment of correspondence awaiting his attention, piles of books not yet reshelved, boxes of canned goods and pasta ready to be taken to the food pantry, and a bowl full of cough drops and cough drop wrappers. A choir of angels fashioned of empty detergent bottles, felt, and glitter surrounded him. The Sunday-school teacher whose young charges created the angels warned Luke that he had better leave them in his office until after Christmas or he was going to have a very disappointed group of third-grade artists on his hands.

On the home front, his wife Laurie was working overtime. She had her hands full with their three-year-old daughter, Phoebe, who had plunged energetically into the spirit of the season. During the last two weeks, Phoebe insisted upon wearing a yellow paper crown everywhere she went, happily pretending to be one of the "Fweeh Kings of Oweeantah." Laurie's ears were beginning to regret teaching Phoebe how to sing "Jingle Bells." Her little bundle of high-pitched exuberance was testing the depth of Laurie's patience.

Laurie also tutored special-needs children at a nearby elementary school because she loved the work and because Luke's salary was just barely adequate. Children everywhere were experiencing something of a December focus problem, and her students were definitely no exception. Adding to these responsibilities, Laurie was earning angel wings by helping Luke with the last-minute requests for assistance that always arrived in the wild, needy days before Christmas. Luke was very grateful for his wife's joyful willingness to help.

The kind of help Luke needed right now, however, was nothing short of divine. He took a deep breath, prayed for a miracle, and opened the scriptures assigned for tomorrow. "Second Samuel! What's Christmasy about Second Samuel?" he said aloud to God. Then he hunkered down and looked at the text. "Okay, here we go.

Rest from enemies. Building a house. House of cedar. A place for the people. Where is it?" Not seeing anything sermon-worthy in Second Samuel, Luke discontinued his rambling chatter with God (who he sincerely hoped was listening) and flipped to the gospel lesson. It was the Gospel according to Luke, for whom he was named, and it was the story of Mary grappling with the news that she would give birth to One who would be called Child of the Most High. "What have we got here?" he asked the Gospel, and then, answering his own question, continued his lonely dialogue. "Angel Gabriel arrives. Perplexity in the face of the holy. Do not be afraid. How can this be? Here am I. Angel departs. Hmmm." Nothing. He espied nothing. Not even a hint of inspiration.

People would be expecting great things tomorrow morning. They wanted to be reminded of the reason for the season, and they wanted that reminder to be compelling, poignant, personal, powerful, not to mention humorous. The phone rang. It was a family: mother, father, and three children. They had packed all of their earthly belongings into an old blue station wagon and had driven halfway across the country on the verbal promise of a job. Having uprooted themselves completely, they discovered upon arrival that there was no work after all. The young family had very little money and no place to stay. Could the church help? The family shelter was being organized none too soon, Luke reflected, and got to work. He set them up in a motel that was accustomed to working with the church on such emergency arrangements. He called the president of the board of deacons and left a message, alerting her to the situation. It was as much as he could do for the moment. He would check in with them later.

Returning to the task at hand, Luke rubbed his temples and whispered to himself, "Think. Think!" The morning newspaper sat on one corner of his desk, and a small article caught his eye. It was about the new year and the birth of a new age. There was definitely no shortage of millennial critique these days. The year 2000 would appear in less than two weeks. Those "in the know" were fully aware that the next thousand-year stretch did not actually begin until 2001, but the very number 2000 stirred the determined masses. Great parties were planned. Armageddon alerts filled cyberspace. Television specials abounded. Every major magazine offered the highlights of the second millennium of the Christian era—the great wars, the great loves, the major plagues, the major discoveries, the formation and reformation of peoples and nations. Perhaps this was his handle: the birth of the infant Jesus and the birth of a new age. It could work. Maybe.

Luke jotted down some thoughts on a blank piece of lined notebook paper. The sermon could be called "What Next?" or "Millennial Musings," or "Manger to Megabytes." Each idea was worse than the last. He wrote, "Looking back, we see God incarnated into the middle of a mortal mess. Peering ahead, we see the same mess updated for a third millennium, and we wonder at the power of the incarnation."

"Now there's a three-snore sermon," he mumbled. He crumpled this unsatisfactory page into a ball and threw it in the direction of the wastebasket. He missed. Staring blankly at the crumpled ball, Luke was startled by the buzzer on the church office door. "What now?"

A woman stood there. It was difficult to tell how old she was. Twenties? Thirties? Maybe even forties? She was thin and grubby with stringy, unkempt, dirty-blond hair and two or three teeth missing. It was quite cold out, yet she was wearing only a sweatshirt—no coat. "I'm sorry to bother you," she said. "I have two little kids, and I don't even have Christmas stockings for them. There are no toys. Another church up the street gave us a ham," she explained, "but would you be willing to help with the kids?" Luke called home: Laurie to the rescue! She was glad to do it. She would gather up some new toys and stuffed stockings and have them delivered on Christmas Eve. Thank God for Laurie, he thought again. What would I do without her?

Fourth Sunday, Year B

Seizing a fresh sheet of lined paper, he went back to work. Think, Luke, think. Okay, back to Second Samuel. What about this idea of God building a house, a home—the irony of God making a place for us to rest, to be secure, while there is no place for Mary to rest and the infant Christ is relegated to a stable? Maybe. But how does it relate? How can I connect the idea with the people sitting in the pew? No ideas—*nada*. Look again, Luke. Something is there, something important, something people need to hear. Where is it?

Some weeks, the sermon came readily as if the message were there all along, a mystery disclosed. All Luke had to do was write it down and preach it. Some messages preached themselves. It seemed to Luke that the incarnation should be one of those messages. Some years, it was. He went over to the file cabinet to see what he had come up with last year and the year before and especially the year before that. He would not preach an old sermon. It was unthinkable. Or was it? Perhaps he could totally overhaul an oldie-but-goodie. But before he reached the file cabinet, the phone rang again. It was Laurie this time and not, thank heavens, another cry for help. He was glad to hear her familiar and comforting voice. She said, "Sweetie, I know you're awfully busy, but the Hardings have invited us for drinks and dinner tonight. You could use a break. What do you think?"

The Hardings were the wealthiest family in the church, and they had been teasing Luke with the notion of footing the bill for a desperately needed new roof. Luke hated the idea of groveling at anyone's feet, but a new roof! It would save him heaven knows how many hours of trying to find the money in other ways. It would save the congregation from one more haranguing appeal. "Tell them we would love to come," Luke said. Laurie told him that a very special person wished to have a word with him. "It's me, Daddy!" Phoebe declared with a giggle. "Come home now!" Luke told his little girl he would be home as soon as he could. Laurie gently retrieved the receiver from Phoebe and asked Luke how it was coming. He told her the distressing truth. Laurie then expressed utter confidence in her husband and left him to his scattered contemplations.

"Read it again," Luke spoke to his soul, "it's in there somewhere." He looked heavenward, raising up both hands in a gesture of desperation. "Any time, God," he supplicated, "any time." Luke was interrupted yet again, this time by the janitor, who always came in on Saturday to make sure things were in reasonable shape for Sunday morning. The janitor witnessed Luke's desperate plea. He chuckled and said, "I thought you guys only worked one hour a week." Ordinarily Luke could muster the semblance of a sense of humor for that tired old joke, but not today. He groaned.

The janitor told him there was some bad news. Luke followed him outside to the back of the church building, where someone had spray-painted in bright red and green, "THE END IS NEAR!" "Well, that is bad news," Luke said to the janitor. Together, they glared disapprovingly at the vandalism. One of those kooks who was convinced that somehow the number two thousand signaled the second coming or the judgment day or some other version of impending doom had taken it upon himself (or herself, he thought to be fair) to spread the word. Luke told the janitor that there was not really much that could be done about the paint now. He would have to deal with it next week or maybe even after Christmas. His head started to pound.

While they stood there shivering, a funny-looking, bearded old fellow walked through the churchyard toward them. It was Wesley. Wesley showed up every couple of weeks looking for food. "Is that true?" Wesley asked, looking intently at "THE END IS NEAR!" "Well, the end is coming eventually. It's just good physics," responded Luke, who strongly suspected that Wesley had no idea what he was talking about. Luke removed a five-dollar bill from his wallet and sent Wesley on his way. Luke and Wesley had a deal with a local diner. Wesley always spent Luke's money on food at this diner and not on anything else, because he knew Luke would check up on him.

Luke went to the sanctuary and sat down in the second pew. Everything looked lovely. The deep purple paraments were in place. A beautiful Advent wreath on a wrought iron pedestal stood ready for the lighting of the fourth candle. A thick fir tree covered with white Crismon ornaments was placed to one side of the room. The space was quiet and lovely, and Luke wished it were Thursday or Friday or even six hours ago. He retrieved a pew Bible from its appointed place in front of him and looked again at Second Samuel. This time, the words practically leapt off the page: "I have been with you wherever you went." Those words were as fresh and true today as they were two thousand years ago and long before that. "I have been with you wherever you went." There was no point in the entire history of humanity when God had abandoned the creation.

"It's just that we don't always realize it, God" he said, hearing his voice echo in the empty sanctuary. That is why we need the incarnation, he thought, because we do not always recognize the presence of God. We think we are alone when we are not. We think things are out of control when they are not. We think the page is blank when, in fact, it is full.

Slowly, thoughtfully, Luke returned to his chaotic-looking desk and to the waiting page. The words came to him quickly now. He could not write as fast as they sprang to consciousness. His own distracted brainwork was overshadowed by higher thoughts. "I have been with you wherever you went." This was a message about sacred love meeting human hope, a message of divine patience and grace, a message of unconditional companionship. The message made him think of all the times in his own life when, without his knowing it until much later, God had led him, directed him, provided for him, blessed him. These leadings and directions and provisions and blessings often arrived in surprising and unexpected ways, even as the Savior arrived in a startling and wondrous manner.

When he was almost finished, Luke turned again to the gospel story. More words jumped out at him. "Nothing will be impossible with God." This is true, he thought. With God, nothing is impossible. He responded to the words by borrowing Mary's prayer and offering it anew. "Here am I, the servant of God; let it be with me according to your word." The phone rang again and, with a renewed understanding of God's presence and direction, Luke readied himself for the next request.

Questions for Reflection and Discussion

1. Why was Luke's life so busy? Why is Advent such a busy time?
2. Both children and adults experience a "focus" problem in December. Do you have any ideas for helping people to focus on Advent as a period of preparation for the incarnation?
3. What prompts the anxiety and craziness of millennialism? Why are some people stuck in a message of impending doom? Is there anything to be gained from such a sense of urgency?
4. Luke wrote, "Looking back, we see God incarnated into the middle of a mortal mess. Peering ahead, we see the same mess updated for a third millennium, and we wonder at the power of the incarnation." What power does the incarnation hold over your life? Over the world?
5. Luke struggled to connect the idea of holy rest with the people in the pew. Any ideas?
6. Luke was busy, but he agreed to join the Hardings for dinner. Was he right to do so?
7. Luke feels called to the message "I have been with you wherever you went." Have you experienced the presence or direction of God? How so?
8. Mary's prayer (Luke 1:38) constitutes a letting go. Did Luke let go and let God? How so?

Fourth Sunday, Year B

The Wait

Jeremiah 33:14–16, Luke 21:25–36

—

The days are surely coming, says God, when I will fulfill the promise I made to the house of Israel and the house of Judah.

⤺ Jeremiah 33:14

Be on guard so that your hearts are not weighed down with dissipation and drunkenness and the worries of this life, and that day catch you unexpectedly, like a trap. For it will come upon all who live on the face of the whole earth. Be alert at all times.

⤺ Luke 21:34–36a

It was December 3, Mildred's birthday, and she was absolutely certain that if she sat in the leather lounge chair next to the phone, eventually her son would call. So she sat there, reclined actually, with a stack of reading material that could last a week or more. In the stack were three back issues of *Maturity World,* two *Literary Digest*s, one *Architectural Lines* magazine, this month's church newsletter, and a 432-page novel she had checked out of the library on Wednesday. In a very unfocused manner, Mildred picked up a *Literary Digest* and flipped through its familiar pages. It was almost ten o'clock in the morning.

67

Before completely settling into the trenches, she decided that another cup of coffee might be necessary. Retreating to her kitchenette, she chose a mug festooned with a majestic peacock in full feather, spooned some instant coffee crystals into it, and waited for the kettle to complete its mission. As she stood there wondering why it is that a watched pot never does boil, she gathered a few butter cookies onto a plate, adding them to her arsenal. Secure in her preparations, Mildred again advanced to the low-slung lounge chair.

No sooner had she selected an article (she chose one about the degeneration of public schools) than the phone rang, or rather buzzed. She wished it rang, but the phones that came with this apartment were all buzzers, and Mildred could not justify spending good money on a replacement just for the pleasure of a good old-fashioned ring.

Not wanting her son to think she was just sitting there waiting for his call, she let it buzz three times before grasping the receiver. Before offering her usual formal "Hello," she glanced at the clock on the wall, noting its time: 10:10. Not bad, she thought. Maybe in middle age he is getting better at remembering his poor old mother.

Mildred's son Garrett (a family name) had recently remarried after a long and drawn-out but not particularly nasty divorce. Joint custody of Adam was readily negotiated. The sticky divorce issues concerned division of a lovely collection of antique clocks, which the couple had acquired over a period of fifteen years. Mildred missed Garrett's first wife but not too much. She did not like his second wife at all. Mildred thought she was too needy. She worried, too, that the second wife would not give young Adam the attention he so desperately needed.

Convinced that Garrett was at the other end of the birthday line, Mildred was greatly disappointed to hear the bold, raspy, former-cigarette-smoking voice of her second-floor neighbor Edna. Edna was just the opposite of everything Mildred treasured in a human being.

She was loud. She was fat—well, not fat really, but certainly lumpy in a most unattractive way. She was overly friendly and virtually without taste. Her scatterbrained tendencies were pronounced.

"Good morning, Millie!" an offensively exuberant voice announced to a furtively bristling Mildred. No one had ever called Mildred "Millie." It was unthinkably cute. Mildred had not yet determined how, gently yet firmly, to correct Edna. "Good morning, Edna," came the aloof reply. "Listen, honey." Mildred shuddered. "I'm having a little luncheon here today. I've invited the Vietnamese cleaning ladies. They are so nice, don't you think? They really are." Edna always answered her own questions. She continued, "Ruth Hoffrau from the third floor is going to teach us how to make Christmas ornaments out of those funny little things. What do you call them? They're not pine cones. Edna, you're losing your mind." That happened long ago, judged Mildred. "Teasels," Edna erupted, "they're teasels! Can you imagine? Well, you know Ruth. She's so clever. Anyway, we're going to make Christmas raccoon ornaments out of teasels and take them over to the children's home. You know, brighten the place up a bit. I'd love for you to come. I'm serving cream of mushroom soup with fresh biscuits."

There was the slightest pause in Edna's bouncy soliloquy, and Mildred—who could imagine nothing worse that spending her birthday afternoon making raccoon ornaments out of teasels—fired off a quick response. "I'm sorry, Edna, but I am terribly busy today and I hate to cut short our conversation but I am expecting an important phone call." Out of her profound sense of the importance of politeness, she added, "but I do thank you for your thoughtful invitation." Mildred hoped she did not sound rude and immediately regretted using the phrase "important phone call" as if Edna's phone call were not. She wanted, however, to be perfectly clear that she was not going to any soup-and-biscuit Christmas raccoon teasel party—with the cleaning ladies, no less!

First Sunday, Year C

Jarred from her position, Mildred once again settled into the lounge chair. She gave up on the *Literary Digest* article, moving to the church newsletter, which had arrived only yesterday. She struggled to remove the wicked little staple that held the folded papers together. Did the church not know how difficult it was for a mature farsighted person to remove those uncooperative staples? She almost always wound up piercing herself or ripping the newsletter or both.

The pastor's letter addressed the subject of waiting. "Dear Friends," he wrote, which always bothered Mildred because, while she held the pastor in fairly high regard, they were certainly not friends and were not likely to become such.

> Dear Friends,
>   Advent is a time of patient waiting and expectant watching: waiting for salvation, watching for signs of God's coming into the world anew. In the midst of the seasonal glitter, may you be alert to God's presence and call in your life.
>   Sincerely and with Love in Christ,
>   Gerald Smith

Mildred had no "seasonal glitter" in her apartment. She thought it pointless to decorate the house for herself alone. She did have a box of Christmas things in the back of her bedroom closet and wondered if she should donate these to the children's home, where the poor tortured teasels were headed. If she wanted to see Christmas decorations, all she had to do was go to the mall.

Mildred perused the church newsletter and moved into *Architectural Lines*. Her husband, George, had been an architect, and while he had not made a lasting impression in the field, he had been a dependable member of a reputable firm until his retirement ten years ago. They were given just over one year to enjoy that retirement before George died, quite unexpectedly, of a heart attack. For the very first time in her life, Mildred was on her own. She felt cheated.

Halfway through a rather dry but interesting article about famous architectural plans that were never executed, the phone buzzed again. Once more Mildred waited until the third buzz to pick it up. The clock read 10:52. She dearly hoped it would be Garrett with his birthday wishes, but it was some woman she did not even know asking for her help in the soup kitchen. Apparently, a ghastly virus had struck more than half of the regular soup kitchen volunteers, and the caller, who identified herself as the "soup kitchen coordinator," was desperate for help.

"Excuse me, how did you get my name?" Mildred inquired decorously.

"Your pastor recommended you," the woman answered brightly.

Oh great, thought Mildred, with no small amount of annoyance in her heart. My "friend." She glared at the church newsletter on the floor. Mildred oh-so-graciously declined the invitation and, upon hanging up, ate one of the butter cookies in her immediate supply. Then, having been interrupted, she dropped the article, took the phone off the hook, and set out to deal with the predictable effects of two large cups of coffee. She did have an answering machine but did not want Garrett to think she was out. With the line busy, he would know to call back.

Mildred was getting tired of hoisting herself in and out of the frustrating lounge chair, but down she went again, reclaiming the *Architectural Lines* and locating the place where she had stopped. She made it through another page and a half before she dozed off. This happened all too often. But at the age of sixty-eight, Mildred figured cat naps to be both normal and allowable.

It was nearly noon when her nap was interrupted, again by the buzzing phone. She had been dreaming that she was in a soup kitchen. The funny thing, however, was that instead of holding the ladle, she was holding up, with both hands, an empty bowl.

It was Edna again—Edna and her teasels. Mildred rolled her bleary eyeballs. "Millie," said the cheery voice, "I'm hoping your day has cleared up a bit, because I've set a place for you. One of the cleaning ladies, Nellie, you know Nellie? Of course you do. Well, Nellie is bringing French pastries from the new bakery, the one that is run by that nice Vietnamese family, and I would just love it if you could come."

"Edna." It was all Mildred could think to say while she tried to conjure a nice way of declining the invitation again. She took a deep breath.

Interpreting her tentative response as a yes, Edna continued, "Oh that's great, Millie! Listen, don't bring a thing. Just yourself. Oh, and you might want to bring an apron just so you don't get glue from the teasels on your clothes. See you in about half an hour. Nothing fancy, mind you. Oh, I'm so glad you're coming. Wait till you see these adorable raccoons."

What was she to do now? She still had not heard from Garrett. Mildred fretted for a few minutes, considering her options. She could call Garrett herself. She could call back the persistent Edna right away and explain that she really could not possibly come. She could wait a few minutes and feign sudden sickness. All of these options felt awkward to her. She chose the last.

Mildred could concentrate on nothing but the clock as she waited anxiously for enough time to have passed to offer a convincing illness. In the meanwhile, she called upon her reserves of spirit to fight off that unique sadness which is central to the experience of being forgotten. At 12:21, she picked up the phone to call Edna and, with the receiver in her hand, Mildred experienced a sudden change of heart. So what if Edna was too loud! So what if the cleaning ladies scarcely spoke English! So what if she had no knack whatsoever for arts and crafts and felt strongly that teasels belonged in compost bins, not on Christmas trees! At least she would not be alone. She would show Garrett that she had a life of her own, even if it were not much of one.

Still feeling surprised at herself, Mildred abandoned the fort and went down to Edna's second-floor apartment. The event in every way met her expectations. Edna's apartment could be an advertisement for holiday decorating mistakes. The soup was right out of a can. The biscuits were overbaked, and she served them with a gloppy, low-fat butter substitute. Edna was loud. Mildred had a terrible time understanding the cleaning ladies. Ruth Hoffrau managed to get her through three very silly-looking teasel raccoons. (Ruth insisted she take one home with her, which Mildred did.)

However, the teasel event also exceeded Mildred's expectations. A few wonderful things actually happened there. Edna, in her rolling conversation, kept using the expression "Count your blessings," and after a short while, Mildred began in her own mind to review her blessings. She remembered they were many. Among them she counted her health, her remarkable memories, the ways in which her good husband had loved and provided for her, the fact that her son and his family (for all their troubles) were reasonably happy and productive human beings. She found herself unexpectedly grateful for the small things, too. The French pastries, which were surely the closest thing she would get to a birthday cake that day, were exquisite. The smiles on the faces of the cleaning ladies, whom she now knew personally as Nellie and Hannah, were lovely and, she found, contagious. Ruth Hoffrau was the picture of patience with Mildred, who proved, once again, that she was indeed all thumbs. And Edna, for all her oddness, held a kindness and generosity of spirit that were downright inspiring.

Back in her apartment, Mildred checked the answering machine, which as yet held no birthday felicitations. She looked over at the lounge chair and felt a little ridiculous about the way in which she had spent the morning waiting in the worst way. She felt foolish for being so resistant to the idea of working in the soup kitchen and pondered the idea of calling them back to volunteer. Perhaps she would. Perhaps tomorrow she would trade in her empty bowl for a full ladle. She spied the church newsletter on the floor next to the lounge chair, retrieved it, and reviewed the pastor's letter. She thought again about patient waiting and expectant watching and being alert to God's presence and call in her life.

Mildred found a piece of red yarn in her sewing basket and tied the funny little teasel raccoon to a ring at the center of her living room lighting fixture. Then she laughed at it openly and left it to brighten the room. The teasel seemed replete with meaning. It was a birthday present. And a Christmas present. It was a reminder that sitting like a blob in a lounger is no way to experience the realm of God. It was a symbol that it is possible, after all, to teach an old dog new tricks. It was a sign that in spite of her son's neglect, in the remarkably diverse family of God, Mildred was not forgotten.

Questions for Reflection and Discussion

1. What were Mildred's reasons for disliking Edna? Do you think those were her deepest reasons? Think of someone whom you dislike. Do you hold anything in common with this person?
2. Why was Mildred so appalled at the luncheon invitation? Why did she change her mind? Have you ever attended an event reluctantly only to be surprised by joy?
3. Why did Mildred object so strenuously to being called a "friend" by the pastor? To what did the pastor refer in using this word? Describe the meaning of Christian friendship.
4. Why did Mildred choose not to decorate her apartment? Can decorations be useful? How?
5. Why do you think Garrett did not call? Will he?
6. How long do you think it had been since Mildred counted her blessings? How does it happen that a human being forgets to be grateful? What prompts thankfulness?
7. Do you think Mildred called the soup kitchen the next day to volunteer? Why or why not?
8. What did Mildred learn about waiting? How are we called to wait for God?

Silver and Gold

Malachi 3:14, Luke 3:1–6

—

But who can endure the day of his coming, and who can stand when he appears? For he is like a refiner's fire and like fullers' soap; he will sit as a refiner and purifier of silver, and he will purify the descendants of Levi and refine them like gold and silver, until they present offerings to God in righteousness.

> Malachi 3:2–3

The word of God came to John son of Zechariah in the wilderness. He went into all the regions around the Jordan, proclaiming a baptism of repentance for the forgiveness of sins.

> Luke 3:2b–3

*M*arty did not feel as sick as he truly was. In fact, other than a little shortness of breath, he felt great. The doctors had been brutally honest with him, however. He needed triple bypass surgery, and he needed it soon. Although he was a third-generation American, years of eating like a good Austrian boy had caught up with Marty: all those delicious wursts, all that wonderful butter and cheese, all that rich cake—all that fat! His wife never rose to the level of magnif-

icent cooking that his mother consistently offered, but she was never
far from it. Since her death, Marty had taken up cooking himself and
was not half bad. But the wild cholesterol ride was over, and Marty
set out for the undiscovered land of unadorned vegetables. His was a
systemic purge, a crash course in digestive purification. Suddenly he
was learning to like spinach without the cream, green beans without
the bacon bits, and an assortment of verdant delicacies he had never
before attempted: artichokes, zucchini, escarole.

Beyond mere dietary changes, this nosedive into the realm of his
own mortality sent Marty into a sweeping reassessment of his inner
life and his outer relationships, particularly with his family. It was a
strange time of year to be going through all of this—right before
Christmas. It appeared to Marty that the world was busily going
mad with superficialities while he was being driven, against his will,
deeper and deeper into his soul. He believed that until this time, he
had never fully understood the meaning of soul-searching. Tears had
never come easily to Marty, but ever since his precarious condition
was revealed to him, he found himself intermittently weeping. And
while he was not known as a particularly religious man, more and
more frequently he found himself lost in prayer.

Marty's wife, Hazel, had died years ago after a long battle with
cancer. Curiously, she died right around this time of year. Watching
his dear wife die was indescribably dreadful. He coped in the only
way he knew how—by distancing himself from the pain. Many
times since then, Marty wished he had expressed certain things to
Hazel: his gratitude for her patience with him, his undying affection
for her, his admiration of her attentive mothering. Together, they
raised two hardworking daughters, Karen and Brenda, now forty and
forty-two respectively.

At this point in their separate lives, everyone was politely
estranged. Birthday and Christmas cards were exchanged regularly,
but there was no other contact. Marty had played well the part of the
strict and controlling Teutonic father, and this was what he got for it:

two daughters who would not come near him. He questioned why he had not been more tender, but he knew the answer. He understood that he was simply following in his own father's footsteps. Marty loved those girls more than life itself, but expressing that love was not the family way. He continued to carry their baby pictures and their high-school graduation photos in his wallet.

Marty took no comfort from the lamentable fact that Karen and Brenda would have nothing to do with one another either. They had always been fiercely competitive. Looking back, Marty realized that he had encouraged it. He believed the competition would help them to excel, and it probably did, but not without expense. Without leaving the country, they could not have lived farther apart. Marty lived just outside Denver, Karen was an attorney in Tampa, and Brenda had her own computer business in Spokane. Neither daughter was married. Marty suspected this was the ultimate revenge—no grandchildren. Karen, who had apparently spent years in therapy, was very clear in her intentions not to pass on any of her ice-cold family genes. Brenda simply did not have time for relationships, and she was not interested in thinking about her childhood at all. Ever the pragmatist, she saw no point in digging up the past.

Marty did not know for certain when the final falling-out had taken place, but he thought it might have had something to do with a doll, an old plastic doll. After Hazel died, the girls tried to straighten up the house a bit for their father. In sorting through their mother's things, they found a foolish old doll with a pull string that used to make it say things like "I love you" and "You're neat!" Each girl insisted the broken-down doll belonged to her. A screaming match ensued, and Brenda ended up taking the doll home with her. Marty thought the whole thing was ridiculous, but it was, apparently, the last straw in a lifetime of trying to share what there was not enough of.

Karen, the younger, was forever coming in second. Both girls ran track in high school, bringing glory to family and school. It was Brenda, however, who always held the spotlight. Karen looked forward to sisterless junior and senior years, but even then she rarely finished first. From all appearances, Brenda enjoyed pouring salt in Karen's open ego wounds. Hazel often tired of playing the unsuccessful mediator/mom. Perhaps they were better off at opposite ends of the country.

His family life was a snarl, but Marty did have good friends. He had always carefully maintained his friendships. He held a respected place in a long-standing bowling league. He belonged to a community organization that raised funds for brain-injured children. He golfed. He was an upstanding retired citizen who never missed an opportunity to vote and enjoyed discussing politics. Marty was never at a loss for an opinion. He was for gun control and was strongly in favor of stricter immigration laws. He thought schools spent too much money on computers and not enough time on the three R's. He was for stronger protection of the environment and opposed to women in the military. He considered himself to be a reasonable man but had difficulty discussing anything in a civil manner with someone whom he considered to be wrong.

All of these things did not seem to matter anymore. Marty was facing the possibility of death, and suddenly what mattered to him most was his family. These things he confided to his neighbor and perhaps best friend, Roland Compeer. Roland, who had undergone similar surgery two years earlier, was terrifically supportive. He was a great listener who understood better than any of his other friends the internal turmoil Marty was experiencing. What Marty did not know was that Roland took it upon himself to phone the girls. Roland called and told them frankly that their father was gravely ill. Furthermore, he stated that their father would never ask them to come. Nevertheless, he desperately wanted—no, needed—them to be there for the surgery.

The bypass would take place in two days. It all seemed frighteningly routine to the doctors, but it was certainly not routine for Marty, who was, only of necessity, placing his heart in someone else's hands. He was unaccustomed to such discomforting dependencies. He had no choice but to trust in the surgeon's experience and abilities. As the date of the dreaded operation approached, Marty lost more and more sleep. This offered him even more waking hours during which to study his mistakes, embellish his regrets, consider the ways in which he had already bypassed his heart, confess his sins to a God who had been little more than a stranger two weeks ago. He wondered how much more inner contemplation he could endure.

Karen felt torn in two. She was wrapping up a big criminal case. Her defense had gone reasonably well. In fact, she hoped to secure a favorable verdict by tomorrow. Nothing was ever certain, however, in a courtroom. Did her father really need her? Did he need anyone? In any event, there was no way she could leave until the trial was over, and she simply did not know when that would be. She contemplated calling her father but was distressed by the idea. She was afraid flowers would appear to be too funereal, so she sent him a big bouquet of Mylar "Get Well Soon" balloons.

Brenda got off the phone with Roland and blurted out a sharp "Hah!" She could not imagine her father with a broken heart. The next morning, she mused aloud in front of Tracy, her horrified administrative assistant, "How can a man have triple bypass surgery when he doesn't have a heart?" Tracy replied simply, "I'm sorry," which left Brenda feeling embarrassed by her own harshness. Brenda left Tracy and her well-oiled machine of a company with instructions for the next several days and went home to pack. She would drive. She owned a brand-new sport utility vehicle and had been looking for an excuse to break it in. She could scream all the way to Colorado if she liked—try to get it out of her system before she arrived at the hospital. If she left this afternoon, she could find a place to stay in Butte, spend all of Wednesday on the road, find a place near the hospital Wednesday night, and get there bright and early before the surgery. She threw a small bag of necessities into the back seat and then ran back into her house. There she retrieved a very battered-looking doll, which she placed in the passenger seat next to her.

The straight shot through the Bitterroot Range to Butte was an easy run, and Brenda had no trouble finding a decent motel room. Most of the next day was lovely. She blasted a new CD over and over again until she had the lyrics memorized. Twice she called Tracy from the car with business details she had neglected to review prior to her departure. Frequently she had little biting conversations with the doll.

By late afternoon, Brenda encountered some annoying flurries, and by the time she got to Casper, dense patterns of small flakes were pouring down relentlessly from the clouds. Relentless shifted to furious. Brenda was forced to stop in Cheyenne because the police had closed Route 25. More-sensible folks had stopped far sooner and earlier than she. Therefore, most of the beds in Cheyenne were occupied.

Through the magic of cell-phone technology and internet wizardry, Tracy located a room for Brenda in a very quaint and conspicuously expensive place called the Fox Farm Inn. Yards upon yards of fresh evergreen roping were wrapped around every post on the grounds. Bright red chili peppers were wired to the roping to complete the effect. It was after ten o'clock when Brenda finally checked in that night. She was grateful to find that the inn had a small bar, which was full of other weary travelers attempting to warm up their insides.

At the bar, Brenda ended up sitting next to a woman named Christine, who was on her way home to her family in Fort Collins after an insurance conference in Rock Springs. Inevitably the subject turned to parents, and Brenda spoke of her uncomfortable predicament. In the strange and sometimes strangely just ways of God's universe, Christine revealed the loss of a younger brother in a tragic automobile accident. She spoke to Brenda wistfully, saying, "There's no time, you know, for pettiness in this life. It can be altogether too brief." Hers was a wisdom born of grief.

Second Sunday, Year C

Karen was not pleased when the jury offered a confident guilty verdict. She hated losing and had learned to pretend to be gracious about it even when she was not. Her colleague Gabe, who had worked with her on the case, turned to her and humbly asked, "You buyin'?" Karen really did not feel like company tonight, but this was a tradition. Win or lose, lead counsel buys the "ultimate nachos" at Victor's, a local courthouse hangout. For a losing attorney to shirk this customary responsibility displayed poor sportsmanship.

Small, blinking Christmas lights were strung along the wainscoting of Victor's. Wreaths formed of Spanish moss adorned the doors. The pub mascot, a golden retriever named Pinkerton (the only one in the pub who was trusted absolutely), was curled up in his usual corner sporting a red and green bandanna for the season. Karen went over to greet Pinkerton before settling down with Gabe. Over a heaping plateful of cheese-laden nachos, Karen explained her family situation to Gabe, who was surprisingly unsympathetic. "Just go," he said intensely; "you might be sorry if you don't."

Karen explained that it would be a good deal easier if she knew her sister would not be there, to which Gabe responded, "Be fearless, Karen. You're both ten years older. She probably doesn't bite anymore." This brought a much-needed smile to Karen's heart. She abandoned the idea of trying to manufacture a good excuse not to go. She had no excuses. She booked a flight for the next evening and then, having listened to an ominous weather report, decided to switch to a morning flight. It would give her time to poke around Denver, maybe even look up an old friend or two.

Karen was amazed at how much Denver had grown in the time she was gone. She rented a car at the airport but it was too early to check into her hotel, so she spent two hours aimlessly shopping. Bored by this unrewarding activity, she continued her journey west a few more miles until she reached the home in which she had grown up. It looked small. He had changed the color of it, which surprised her. It had always been gray with matching shutters. Now it was a lovely soft blue with white shutters. She took a deep breath and pulled into the driveway.

Marty was shocked to see his daughter. He nearly did not recognize her for she was so grown-up, so sophisticated in appearance. She looked so much like her mother but taller, stronger. The tears in his eyes stunned and melted her. He was not the same man, she could see that. Marty was both embarrassed and delighted to discover that Roland had called Karen. It was a gift he would never forget. The conversation between father and daughter did not flow readily, but it was not as strained as Karen had expected. She was utterly amazed by the wonderful lunch and dinner he fixed for her in his balloon-filled kitchen. This used to be her mother's space—exclusively. Karen was also amazed to find that her sister was not yet there. She had arrived first. Perhaps it was a paradigm shift, a sign of change.

The roads were reopened by morning, the landscape blanketed by glistening snow. Brenda, who was exhausted from the harrowing journey and from very little sleep, took her time in leaving Cheyenne. She met Christine once more before she left, at the coffeepot next to the front desk. Brenda wished her a good trip home, and Christine said a funny thing that would keep Brenda's mind occupied the rest of the way to Denver. "Bitterness is a prison that masquerades as a fortress," she said.

By the time Brenda got to the hospital, her father was in the operating room, on his way to a more functional heart. She met Karen in the waiting room, said nothing, but handed her sister the old doll that had kept her company all the way from Spokane. Karen reached out and graciously took the gift. It had been such a long time. Gabe was right. They were both ten years older and, hopefully, ten years wiser. Brenda, like her father, noted the remarkable resemblance between Karen and their mother.

Second Sunday, Year C

Brenda and Karen, as they waited for word of their father, spent several hours becoming reacquainted and beginning the often awkward process of forgiveness. The waiting-room walls were covered with Christmas cards sent by grateful patients. With hours on their hands, they read these cards studiously. Brenda and Karen were struck by three messages in particular. One card read, "All flesh shall see the salvation of God." The second, "Glory to God in the highest heaven, and on earth peace among those whom God favors." The third card said in big bold letters, "May God give you a heart of love for Christmas." Long after Marty had recovered, Brenda would reflect to Karen that the surgery turned out to be quite a bargain because all three of them got new hearts out of one operation—hearts from which the plaque of resentment had been removed, hearts ready to forgive and eager to be forgiven, hearts of love for Christmas and beyond.

Questions for Reflection and Discussion

1. Facing mortality, Marty began to reassess his life. What else prompts inner searching?
2. There were words Marty wished he had imparted to Hazel while she was alive. What holds a person back from such expressions? Are there words you are withholding from a loved one?
3. Was Marty responsible for the enmity between his daughters?
4. Why did Brenda and Karen have such a terrible falling-out over a plastic doll? How is it that molehills become mountains?
5. Why did Karen continue to finish in second place after her sister left home? Is it possible to break out of entrenched family patterns?
6. Did Roland Compeer interfere in his friend's life by calling Marty's daughters? Have you ever felt called to step in where you were not sure you belonged? What happened?

7. What role did Gabe and Tracy play in the daughters' decisions to visit their father? Were they divine messengers? Have you ever been positively influenced by an unsympathetic ear?
8. Why is forgiveness so difficult and so holy?

Festival Day

Zephaniah 3:14–20, Luke 3:7–18

—

Your God is in your midst, a warrior who gives victory;
God will rejoice over you with gladness, you will be
renewed in God's love; God will exult over you with
loud singing as on a day of festival.

> Zephaniah 3:17–18a

And the crowds asked John, "What then should we do?"
In reply he said to them, "Whoever has two coats must
share with anyone who has none; and whoever has food
must do likewise."

> Luke 3:10–11

The new minister was a young woman named Mary, fresh out of
seminary—the only type this congregation could afford, and the
only kind willing to take on a dying church with a crisis budget.
Once upon a time, it was the big-steeple church in the neighborhood, full of noteworthy members, most of whom lived nearby. The
congregation that remained comprised faithful older members, most
of whom drove in from safer suburbs out of a sense of obligation or
because they truly loved this place so full of sacred memories. Three
of the church members, all women, objected to the idea of hiring a

female pastor. They thought "she would be unsafe in this neighborhood," which was their code language for "a woman can't do this kind of work." Mary arrived in July with all sorts of exuberance and uncustomary ideas, the very sound of which made many of the church members nervous.

Some of the elders witnessed the writing on the wall years ago and had made well-meaning attempts to meet the needs of a much-changed neighborhood. They started a food pantry and a clothing closet, but these were largely unsuccessful efforts because, while church members kept bringing in contributions, the word did not make it out into the neighborhood. Two large, unused Sunday-school classrooms remained filled with things like warm coats and canned soup.

Without any significant cooperation from the membership, Mary went about introducing herself to the neighbors, many of whom spoke very broken English and some of whom displayed open disdain for a freckle-faced minister invading their neighborhood. After a while, however, some of these neighbors started coming to church—at first out of curiosity, and then because she was not a half-bad preacher for a white woman. The old-timers were so pleased that the church was starting to grow again, they started paying more attention to her thoughts.

Then Mary had the bright idea that during Advent, sometime fairly close to Christmas, they should have a party after church and invite all of the neighbors to come. They could serve a turkey dinner and sing Christmas carols and give presents to the neighborhood children. When she presented her idea to the elders, however, they were more than a little hesitant. They wanted to know who was going to do all of the cooking and where the presents would come from and, most important, who was going to clean up the mess when it was all over. One of them said, with his eyes full of fire, "Look, Mary, we're trying to keep up with you here, but you're just plain moving too fast for us. Maybe we're not ready for you."

Mary was so mad about the wet-blanket reaction, she boldly announced that she was going ahead with the party no matter what. Even if she had to do all the cooking and present buying and cleaning up by herself, there was going to be a party. Even if she was moving too fast for them, which she did not think was true, and even if no one else from the church showed up, there was going to be a neighborhood Christmas party after church. Right then and there, she set a date—the third Sunday in Advent. Then she stormed out of the meeting and left the elders to their incensed sputterings. Mary felt ashamed of her flagrant impatience, but she was tired of banging her head against a wall with these people. She had endured four months of whining, four months of criticism, four months of frustration. "One sign of hope," she prayed, "just give me one sign of hope."

The next day, God, whose extravagance never ceased to amaze Mary, sent not one but three clear signs. Old Zeke McAfee, whose grandparents were charter members of the church and who was one of the worst offenders when it came to resisting the pastor, called Mary at home and offered to cook the turkeys. He even offered to buy them and wanted to know how many she thought they might need. Florence King, one of the three women who did not vote to hire Mary, stopped by the office after her prayer group ended and told the pastor that she had heard all about the party and, while she did not think it would be well attended, the women of the prayer group were prepared to buy new children's books, wrap them up, and have them ready. If no children showed up, they would contribute the books to the neighborhood library, which could certainly use the donations. Finally, John Morgan, one of a few people in Mary's support system, came by and volunteered to lead a clean-up committee. Mary sent up a sincere "thank you."

She had five hundred flyers printed, hoping for a 10 percent response. She left these around the neighborhood, and, wherever she could, she talked up the event. Then she made appointments with people whom she knew to be leaders in the community. She wanted them to know that this was not about charity—it was about celebration! She received more than a few polite nods and provisional "uh-huhs." With the idealism and energy that are the gifts of youth, she forged ahead, undeterred by cynics, skeptics, and whiners.

As the plans unfolded, a few more church folk stepped up to the challenge offering particular specialties: green bean casserole, squash pie, angel food cake. One of the larger church members, Edward Moore, offered to dress up as Santa Claus. In Mary's book, Santa was only slightly more related to the incarnation than the Easter bunny was related to the resurrection, but she did not want to discourage anyone's efforts or dampen anyone's spirits. The party now had a Santa. There were still plenty of resisters who thought the whole party was overly ambitious or terribly undignified or both, but Mary was pleased with the backing she had received so far.

About a week before the event, which was now being called the "Christmas Festival," a young man called Flash stopped by the church, asking to talk to Mary. Flash said he had a rap group and had written a Christmas song, and he wanted to know if he and his group could perform this rap song at the festival. Mary did not think twice. She gave him an unqualified "yes." She was not sure how to break this news to the elders, the depth of whose reaction would probably be difficult to measure. She decided to wait until later in the week.

During the week, however, once word got out, there were many more requests for time slots in the festival entertainment line-up. A young woman named Naomi wanted to sing her version of "Silent Night." She wanted to know if the church had a piano and a ramp because her sister, who used a wheelchair, was her accompanist. "Yes," answered Mary, "and yes." A group of stomp dancers asked if they could be in the party. "Don't worry about your floor," they said. "We have our own platforms, and we can drag those in the day before." Mary wondered what the elders would think of plywood platforms being dragged onto the recently refinished floor of the fellowship hall. Again she said "yes." An older group of harmony singers felt called to offer their rendition of "O Happy Day." "Yes, yes, yes!" Before she knew it, she had a show on her hands.

On Friday, she called all of the elders and either left messages on their answering machines or tried to gently explain that there was going to be some neighborhood participation. A few of them wanted to know what she meant by "participation," and she simply said, "music." One of the elders said, "You're not fooling anyone, you know." After that phone call, Mary laughed to herself, wondering if maybe she was fooling everyone in the best sense of the word "fool." She hoped so.

Early Saturday morning, Mary threw on an old sweatshirt and some overalls and readied herself for a day of hard work. There were tables to move and places to set and potato salad to make and decorations to hang. Mary wanted everything to say, "Welcome!" She was surprised and relieved to find John Morgan and his daughter Alice, who was visiting for Christmas from Wichita. They had already set tables around the room in a kind of circle. More tables were lined up near the kitchen to be used as a buffet. A church member who had not graced the door of the church for years read about the party in the church newsletter and brought over a large roll of green paper table covering. Bright red poinsettias, which Mary hoped would last through Christmas Eve, served as centerpieces.

The room was looking pretty jolly when the stomp dancers showed up with their equipment. Alice and Mary pushed an old piano, which was (thank heavens) equipped with rolling casters, next to the stomp staging. Flash showed up with an audio system. Two of the prayer group women brought a wicker laundry basket filled with wrapped children's books. They had tied jingle bells all the way around the rim of the basket. John came up with the idea of bringing some of the coats and warmer things downstairs from the clothing pantry and putting a "Free for the Taking" sign on them. He gathered a giant box of winter clothing and placed it just outside the double doors of the community hall. Mary heartily approved.

On the morning of the festival, the church was unusually full. The increased attendance had something to do with the fact that it was so close to Christmas, but it was also prompted by plain old curiosity. People wanted to see what was going to happen after church. Rumors of irreverent activity abounded. Florence King wanted to know if there was really going to be dancing, because, for the record, she was opposed to dancing of any kind in the community hall. Mary asked Florence how she felt about dancing in the sanctuary, to which Florence said, "Well, I never!" Ed Moore was so excited about being Santa that he showed up for church in full costume. Mary was glad he had the good sense to sit in the back row. The church looked very festive. Some of the women had made four bright purple banners with big white felt letters on them reading HOPE, LOVE, PEACE, and JOY. These were placed strategically in each corner of the sanctuary. An old artificial Christmas tree stood in the foyer. Everyone was invited to bring in an ornament to hang on it, and it looked a little plain, but she appreciated the attempt. Perhaps next year they could get a fresh one.

Mary noticed that the hymns were being sung with extra gusto, and she took this as a sign that God was indeed renewing this congregation in love. She offered a spirited message about living a life rich in both humility and expectation. The little church choir was as anemic as usual, but, once again, Mary admired their courage. She watched as a little girl, probably of Korean descent, placed a Christmas card in the offering plate. The service ended with the rousing Welsh hymn "Rejoice, rejoice, believers," and Mary, who was the first to admit that singing was not one of her gifts, threw caution to the winds and openly presented her off-tones.

The festival began cautiously, as people politely filled their plates with a wide variety of special dishes. There was more food than anyone imagined, because neighborhood guests showed up with everything from kimchee to collard greens. As more and more guests arrived, the noise level increased dramatically. Mary watched as Santa went about the room handing the wrapped books to the young children in attendance. She was disappointed to see, however, that church members were sitting with church members, and neighborhood folk were sitting with neighborhood folk. Mary bravely stood up on a chair and asked people to get up and sit next to someone they had never met before. The crowd was reluctant, but many complied, and Mary was gratified to see little conversations springing up between strangers. She knew that most human beings held more in common with one another than they would ever realize.

The program began with a sing-along led by the church choir. This was moderately successful but was certainly not going to win any awards. Next came Flash and his rappers, who offered a tune they called the "Ho Ho Ditty." It had a simple refrain, which they encouraged everyone to say along with them, "Ho ho ho. What d'ya know? What d'ya know?" There was good participation on this one, although it was clear that the older folks of the congregation were more challenged than many others. Ed Moore, who looked as though he was starting to sweat beneath his fake beard, was trying to keep time with his big foot, and Mary, with a big grin on her freckled face, noticed that it simply was not working.

Naomi and her sister offered a sultry and stirring version of "Silent Night" which brought tears to the eyes of some. Then came the stompers. Mary thought the whole thing was remarkable and could not imagine being able to move her feet so fast. Florence King, however, proved how deeply offended she was by walking out on the event. Mary was pleased to see that no one followed her. The final entertainment was delivered by the harmony quartet, which sang, as planned, "O Happy Day." It started softly, slowly with a single tenor voice carrying the tune splendidly. One by one, other voices were added. The tempo picked up gradually until the quartet was singing quite dynamically. The tempo was contagious, and some people got up and started to dance. Mary could scarcely believe her eyes when she saw Old Zeke two-stepping with a little neighborhood girl who looked to be five or six years old. By now, almost everyone was clapping to the beat or at least trying to, and those who knew the words joined in singing the joyful song.

When it was all over, Mary was exhausted and thrilled and very, very grateful to God that the festival was such a big success. Success was not one of her primary goals in life, but she was not about to reject it when it was presented to her. The cleanup did not take nearly as long as she anticipated, because plenty of people stayed to help. Almost all of the warm clothing disappeared from the pile John Moore had put together. A lonely blue glove and a moth-eaten chartreuse cardigan sweater sat in the bottom of the box. Mary stuffed these into a big trash can that was nearly filled with used paper goods.

She remained in the building long after the place was cleaned up and everyone had left. She needed quiet time, time to ponder, time to let the meaning of the moment sink in. Sitting in an old wooden chair and considering the day, Mary noticed a Christmas card lying on her desk. It had a small self-sticking note attached to it from one of the ushers. This read, "Found card in offering plate. Think it's for you." She opened the card in which a young hand had scrawled in crayon, "Merry Christmas Pastor Mary." Mary sighed with satisfaction. She loved her older, sometimes stubborn, always engaging congregation. It was going to be nice, however, to have some younger parishioners, too.

Questions for Reflection and Discussion

1. Do you think the church in this story wanted to grow or not?
2. Why were the elders so resistant to the idea of having a neighborhood Christmas party?
3. Why did Mary object to Santa? What are your feelings about Santa in relation to the celebration of the incarnation?
4. Did Mary enthusiastically invite the neighborhood entertainment out of her desire to build community spirit or to spite the elders? Must our motives be pure in order to be acceptable to God?
5. Why did Mary hope she was fooling everyone in the best sense of the word "fool"?
6. Did God participate in the festival? If so, how?
7. Why did Florence King walk out on the stompers? Do you think, in the long run, she will retain her membership in the church?
8. What will Mary's church look like next Christmas?

Suspension of Disbelief

Micah 5:2–5a, Luke 1:39–45

—

And he shall stand and feed his flock in the strength of God, in the majesty of the name of the Sovereign his God. And they shall live secure, for now he shall be great to the ends of the earth; and he shall be the one of peace.

Micah 5:4–5

"And why has this happened to me?"

Luke 1:43a

"Why is this happening to me?" Zach asked, as he lay stretched out on the couch, his lips pursed, his arms folded tightly against his chest. On the upside-down wooden fruit crate that served as his coffee table sat a half-empty glass of chocolate milk, an unopened jar of roasted cashews his mother had sent a few weeks ago, and a portable phone. Zach had just hung up from another unsatisfactory conversation with his parents, who had, three weeks ago, glibly announced that they were going to Las Vegas for Christmas. They would send him a complete holiday meal from a gourmet catalog.

Furthermore, while they were gone, they were having the whole house painted and recarpeted. In other words, he was not invited to go with them to Las Vegas, and he was not allowed to go home to Florida, either. They had this ridiculous idea that at his age, he should be exercising a little more independence. He was stuck, therefore, in the chilly Northeast for Christmas.

Zach was a senior. He had taken a year off between his sophomore and junior years so that he now felt much older than many of the students around him. "Thank God I have my own place," he said out loud. He had convinced his parents that he was beyond dormitories, which were too noisy to get any work done. By tomorrow, most of the dorms would be closed for the holidays. Where would he be now without his own apartment? When he asked where he was supposed to go on Christmas Day, they suggested he visit his girlfriend, Sue, and her family, who lived a short drive from campus. What his parents did not know, however, was that he had broken up with Sue about a month ago. She was looking for a commitment, and Zach was nowhere near being ready for such a scary leap into the unknown. He would have to sit and eat his gourmet mail-a-meal by himself. "Why?" he asked again. "Why is this happening to me? Who goes to Vegas for Christmas?"

On the Friday before Christmas, as most students were packing up to go home, Zach roused himself from the couch and scanned the newspaper for a movie. He called his good friend Ron, another senior who would be around for the holidays, to see if he wanted "to take in a flick." Ron said he was busy—maybe later. Ron's real name was Ranbir, but he had adapted it to ease confusion. Ron was from India and could not afford to fly home every time there was a school vacation. Zach wondered what Ron did when everyone else went away. He was about to find out. Maybe he would invite Ron over on Christmas Day to share in his mail-order feast.

There were plenty of films from which to choose. There were always new releases at Thanksgiving, which Zach usually avoided because he was too busy writing term papers and studying for exams. Well, as of last Wednesday, this semester was over. Only one more to go. He chose a movie that was described as a sci-fi action thriller. That ought to take his mind off his troubles. But it did not. In fact, some of the thriller was filmed in Vegas, which grated keenly on Zach's nerves. Also, the film required what his contemporary-literature professor frequently referred to as "suspension of disbelief." This reminded Zach that he still could not believe what was happening to him.

Zach had never missed a Christmas at home. His mother always baked a fresh ham, and she made those delicious yams with the marshmallows on top. Then there were the usual traditions—the stockings hung on the banister (like many Floridians, they did not have a fireplace), the presents beneath the tree. Then there was the hunt. Every year, his father left a clue under the Christmas tree. This led to another clue, and so on, until Zach found his big present out in the garage or back by the pool or wherever his parents had conspired to hide it. One year his parents gave him a kitten, which he found hidden in a blanketed box in the coat closet. He still had that kitten, Twinkle. Zach wanted to bring Twinkle back to school with him since he was living in his own place, but his mother talked him out of it. Now, while he spent Christmas in Maine by himself, Twinkle would spend it in the kennel. "What's up with that?" he asked himself.

There was not even any snow. What was the point of spending Christmas in such a cold place when there was no snow? His lousy Christmas was not even going to be a white Christmas. And another thing: How was he supposed to go Christmas shopping? On Christmas Eve, Zach's mother always took him out shopping for his father. Then later that night, when many of his friends were on their way to midnight services at church, his father took him shopping for his mother. This was how it was supposed to be!

On Saturday morning, Zach zipped his ski jacket all the way up to protect his neck from the wintry wind and wandered into the small town, now busy with shoppers, none of them students. Then he walked back through the campus and over to the International House, where Ron lived. He found Ron getting ready to leave for the day. Not thrilled with the idea of spending another minute by himself with nothing to do, he asked Ron, "Where are you going?" Ron answered that he was working on a little project and, noting Zach's forlorn expression, invited Zach to come along. "But you're going to get messy," Ron warned; "go back to your place and put on something you don't care about." He hollered after him, "And bring a hammer if you've got one!"

Without really knowing what he was getting into, Zach went back and threw on his holiest pair of jeans and an old sweatshirt that was tattered around the cuffs of the sleeves, where he had chewed them during a particularly boring thermodynamics lecture. He dragged a toolbox out from beneath the kitchen sink and grabbed the hammer he was given for his thirteenth birthday by his crazy Uncle Phil. Then Zach put his warm jacket back on and drove over to the International House in his baby—his green 1965 Karmann Ghia 1500. Ron, who was trying to keep an old Japanese compact alive through graduation, said, "Okay. You're driving."

The Karmann Ghia was also a birthday gift, this one from his parents on his eighteenth birthday. It remained in pristine condition, much as it looked when his parents first gave it to him. Even when he had no time to breathe because the workload was so heavy, Zach washed and vacuumed the car once a week and kept it covered when not in use. It had black leather seats and mahogany trim on the dash, and while he had hoped for a convertible, this model was equipped with an original electric sunroof. It was an impressive car. Sometimes Zach had the feeling that Sue liked his car more than she liked him, which was interesting because Sue sometimes had the feeling that Zach liked his car more than he liked her. Nothing for either of them to worry about anymore.

"Where are we going?" asked Zach. "Well, we're going to help build a house," Ron said with conviction. As they drove out into the country, Ron explained that he was helping to build a house for a family with two small children and another on the way. Currently they were living in a rented trailer that was not very well insulated and appeared to have a roof problem. The new house was nearly finished, the wiring and rough plumbing in, the windows installed. "Today is Sheetrock day," said Ron. "You will get dusty." When they arrived, there were a few oohs and aahs over the Ghia (Zach was accustomed to these). Then a woman wearing a heavy tool apron directed them to a room upstairs. It was, they were told, a children's room.

The family that would soon become the proud owners of this little house had a six-year-old boy, a four-year-old girl, and a baby due any day now. The father, whose name was Kevin, worked two part-time jobs at close to minimum wage and could never, under ordinary circumstances, afford to own a home. Because the house was being built by volunteers with many donated materials, the mortgage would be small enough for this family to handle. Ron explained to Zach that he would probably meet some of the family members during the day, because they were all helping, too. Construction of the house entailed a partnership between the family and the community, with the family putting in a measured amount of sweat.

"How long have you been working on this?" Zach asked.

"Several weeks," he answered. "There is a little group of students that has been coming over here regularly to work on it."

"And how come I never heard about it?"

"I guess I thought you wouldn't be interested. You don't seem like the construction-worker type."

"Oh, and you do!" Zach blurted out sarcastically. He picked up a loose rag that was lying on the plywood floor and threw it at Ron.

They laughed mightily and got to work. Zach hammered the Sheetrock into place and Ron followed behind taping over the cracks between pieces. The house was cold. The electricity was hooked up, but there was no heat yet except for a couple of little space heaters, which volunteers took turns borrowing from one another. It was early afternoon when they were interrupted by a scruffy little boy, who tugged at the bottom of Zach's sweatshirt. "This is my room," he said proudly. "My bed is gunna go there and my dressah is gunna go there and there's gunna be a toybox and a train track and it's all gunna be ready for Christmas."

"Really!" Zach reacted. "Reeeally," the boy replied.

Ron introduced Zach to Drew and verified Drew's claim.

"Where's all your stuff now?" Zach asked.

"I don't have it yet but it's gunna be here for Christmas."

Ron instructed Drew not to build his hopes up, because they still had a long way to go. The diminutive Drew was insistent, however. He said God had promised him.

"God?" asked Ron.

"Yeah, God. The one who stands up in the church every Sunday and says stuff about love and Jesus and all that."

"I hate to disappoint you, but that's not God," said Ron. "That's just the minister."

"So what!" said Drew and ran off.

"Not shy," Zach commented.

"Not shy at all," added Ron.

Shortly after their surprising conversation with Drew, a young woman who was conspicuously pregnant came to tell them lunch was ready. Every day, lunch was supplied by a different group in the community. Every Saturday, lunch was provided by members of the Congregational church, who had prepared hot chili, fresh bread, sliced carrots and celery, blueberry cake, and plenty of coffee. Zach could not believe how many people were working on the house, all at the same time. There must have been at least two dozen from the looks of the lunch line. Zach ate like a horse, a fact that did not go unnoticed. "Not used to working so hard, huh?" Ron questioned his friend. "Guess not," Zach answered truthfully.

While he was on his second piece of the buttery blueberry cake, Kevin drove up to the house in a big old clunky American car. Zach knew who Kevin was immediately because Drew was a little carbon copy of his father, only without the stubble. Zach was expecting someone significantly older and asked Ron if he knew Kevin's age. Ron figured Kevin to be about twenty-five, maybe even a little younger. This seemed incredible: This guy was only a little older than Zach himself! Not only was he married and working, but he had kids! If Zach had been born to different parents or been offered fewer opportunities . . . Zach had a moment of recognition in which he profoundly understood how fortunate, maybe even how spoiled, he was.

Kevin looked up at the house and said, "I can't believe it. It's almost done." Ron took Kevin aside and told him about their encounter with Drew. Ron thought Kevin should know about his son's unrealistic expectations. He suggested a little father and son heart-to-heart to let Drew know that there was no way his room, or the house for that matter, would be ready for Christmas. Ron was astonished to hear Kevin say, "If that pastor says it'll be ready, well then, I believe him."

Zach had been well insulated from the kind of poverty he was encountering today. He was really interested in meeting the man who had made such an outlandish promise. The house was looking good, but *Christmas?* Christmas was only a few days away. Zach did get to meet the gutsy promise-maker because, about three o'clock, the minister showed up on a noisy motorcycle. He did not look at all like a clergyman. He wore cowboy boots and an old black leather jacket and sported a waxy handlebar mustache.

Ron, who seemed to know just about everyone, introduced Zach to Gordon Carpenter, fondly called "Gordo" or sometimes just "Gord," the minister who had developed and orchestrated the project. Ron explained the Christmas-promise predicament to Gord, who took a deep breath and said, "I may have been a little too optimistic. We're getting close. I think with all this help we could get the inside painted by Monday and the carpet laid on Tuesday. I have furniture for the kids. I even got a new toybox for Kevin. Finishing the house for Christmas is not the problem. Our big obstacle is the oil burner. I kept hoping somebody would donate one, but that hasn't happened. A new one will cost about three thousand dollars, and it will take an act of God to find that much money between now and Christmas." Gordon left to find young Drew, who listened carefully and then just shook his incredulous little head saying, "You're wrong. You're wrong. We're gunna be in this house for Christmas. You promised."

At the end of the day, Zach was amazed at how much had been accomplished. He went through the house room by room and saw that, indeed, every inch of it was ready for paint. He planned to be back with a brush in his hands tomorrow. Right now, however, he wanted to rest. He wanted nothing more than to go back to his place and flop down on the couch and order a pizza. He took Ron back to the International House and went home, grateful for the roof over his head.

Zach slept well and soundly, and the next morning, with the encouragement of the Congregational lunch ladies, he considered visiting their church. He missed the service, however, because somehow, he got the time wrong. When he arrived at eleven on the dot, people dressed in their warmest finery were starting to pour out of the sanctuary. Zach ducked inside anyway to thaw his numb hands. One of the lunch ladies spotted him immediately and dragged him into the church parlor, where a few people were chatting and enjoying home-baked Christmas cookies.

Zach had agreed to meet Ron at 12:30 in order to head back up to the house together. After the cookie break, however, Zach called Ron and told him to go on ahead. He said he had something more important to do. Ron was surprised by the call because Zach had seemed so excited about the project yesterday. Hoping his friend would eventually join him, Ron spent the afternoon painting Drew's room yellow (because that was Drew's favorite color).

Shortly after five o'clock, Gordon Carpenter arrived at the site and gathered all of the volunteers together. He told them that he had wonderful news: He had a check in his hands for four thousand dollars. The check would buy a splendid oil burner and a few lighting fixtures that were still needed. Kevin shrieked, "You did it, Gord! I can't believe it!" Drew whispered to his daddy, "I knew it! I knew it!" What Gordon did not announce, because Drew was standing right there, was that the anonymous donor had stipulated that some of the money be used for a high-quality model-train track.

Zach never did show up that afternoon. After a long afternoon of yellow paint, Ron drove by Zach's apartment and noticed that the green Ghia was not in its appointed place. When he called later to ask why his friend had not made it, Zach said, in a strange and wonderful tone of voice, "I didn't have a ride." These words confirmed what Ron had guessed.

"You know what this means, of course," Ron proclaimed. "The house will be done in time. They will lay the carpet tomorrow or the next day and install the new oil burner on Wednesday."

"I know," Zach responded.

"I can't believe it," Ron said.

"I can," Zach answered. "After all, God promised."

Questions for Reflection and Discussion

1. Zach and Kevin were approximately the same age. Who was more mature? Why?

2. How do you think Zach first felt when Ron told him where they were going? Why did Ron not invite his friend to help sooner?

3. Why was Drew so confident that his house would be ready on time? Have you ever had faith when everyone else was saying "No way"? How did you have such faith?

4. When he first met Kevin, Zach recognized how fortunate he was. Do you think this was the first time Zach understood his own earthly advantages? Was God at work here? How?

5. Was Gordon Carpenter wrong to make such promises to Drew?

6. When do you think Zach first had the idea to sell his Karmann Ghia? What will his parents say when they find out?

7. How was Kevin insulated from poverty? Are you? If so, why and how are you insulated?

8. What did Zach mean when he said, "I can't believe this is happening?" What did Kevin mean when he said it? Ron? Elizabeth? (See text from Luke.)

Good News of Great Joy

Isaiah 9:2–7, Luke 2:1–20

—

For a child has been born for us, a son given to us; authority rests upon his shoulders; and he is named Wonderful Counselor, Mighty God, Everlasting Father, Prince of Peace.

> ⏵ Isaiah 9:6

Joseph went to be registered with Mary, to whom he was engaged and who was expecting a child. While they were there, the time came for her to deliver her child. And she gave birth to her firstborn son and wrapped him in bands of cloth, and laid him in a manger, because there was no place for them in the inn.

> ⏵ Luke 2:5–7

*T*he Harrigan family wanted very much to bring the Christmas story to life this year. Rachel and Tom Harrigan wanted their boys to understand what it might have been like for Mary and Joseph and the infant Jesus to take such a long journey and land in somebody's stable because there was no room anywhere else. Rachel's first instinct at the beginning of Advent was to go out and buy the biggest and most realistic manger scene she could find and place it in the middle of the living room so that the whole family would have no choice but to focus on the story. The very presence of the manger would work its way into their deepest reflections.

The Harrigans had two boys, Peter and Simon. Peter was a tenth-grader, a very good student when he applied himself. It was becoming more and more difficult for him to focus, between girls and sports and driver education. Some would say that Simon, now in eighth grade, was following nicely in his brother's footsteps while others would argue that Simon was blazing his own unique path. They were both very determined young men.

The whole Harrigan family was in the thick of basketball season. Peter played center on the JV team (he was a terrific rebounder) and Simon was a point guard (well respected for his ball-handling skills). The Harrigans spent a lot of time at basketball games these days, which was fun for all of them and downright amazing to Tom and Rachel, who as children were not exactly known for their athletic ability. More than once at these games, as they watched their children with endless fascination, they would discuss the mysterious ways in which God advances miraculous genetic leaps.

At this point in their lives, Rachel and Tom carried a dawning concern that their children develop a deeper understanding of their Christian beliefs. They all attended Sunday school with regularity. They knew their kids had a fairly good grasp of the major Bible stories (which was more than could be said for many), and Peter was now a confirmed member of the church. What Rachel and Tom did not yet see in their children were the deeper things, a sense of awe at the creation, an understanding that they could turn to God in all things, a desire to reach out beyond themselves to neighbors in need. They wanted Peter and Simon to move to the next level in their faith, to the place where the rubber meets the road, where assumptions become actions.

Christmas Eve, Years A, B, and C

When a very enthusiastic Rachel went on the major manger search, she came home empty-handed and disappointed. Oh, there were plenty of products from which to choose. A wide variety of manger scenes were available in gift shops everywhere at this time of year. There were the standard nativity sets made of lovely olive wood or pretty porcelain or more-durable plastic. She was also surprised to find sets hammered of tin and formed from pine cones. There were silver mangers, brass mangers, corn cob mangers, even dried bean mangers. She felt, however, that all of them seemed too unreal. They were too clean, for one thing. Rachel figured that a manger would not be a particularly clean place. And some of them were cold. The porcelain figures felt ice-cold in her hands. And none of them were large enough. The dimensions in her head far exceeded standard commercial shelving.

Tom assured his wife that there must be a better way to bring the story to life. While he did not have any bright ideas, he was confident that Rachel would come up with something. She always did. Rachel was one of the most creative people he had ever met. It was part of what he loved so much about her. While she could be a little too optimistic, she seemed to be possessed of an inexhaustible stream of interesting notions.

Rachel's next thought was to go to the public library and immerse herself in Christmas literature. She did not expect to find *the* idea there but hoped that a book or two might trigger a few good thoughts. She picked up a collection of Dickens's Christmas stories, which reminded her of the poor in their community. Perhaps a gift to a poor family. She looked at a few children's Christmas stories, but these were primarily Santa-focused. She supposed that was to be expected. The idea of Santa set her thinking about Christmas traditions from other countries, and she went in search of a resource in this vein. She found three interesting books that described various customs from around the globe.

Many Christmas customs had to do with gift-giving or special foods or interesting little games. These, she thought, were very nice but did not have much to do with the story of Jesus' birth. She liked the Scandinavian practice of thoroughly cleaning the house in preparation for the Christ child but did not think she could sell it to any of her men. Besides, such an idea would meet her own needs more than it would meet the goal of bringing the Christmas story to life.

Rachel was much taken with a tradition from Mexico called *Las Posadas,* which means "the resting places." Through this compelling ritual, the Mexican people remember how difficult it was for Mary and Joseph to find shelter in Bethlehem. By December 16, participants have their homes prepared and decorated. Every home has a nativity scene in it. Neighbors divide themselves into two groups, cruel innkeepers and wandering pilgrims, who carry candles to light their way. Then each home is approached as if it were the inn. A well-known dialogue takes place between the innkeepers and the pilgrims. It goes something like this:

"Who is knocking on my door so late at night?"

"We are weary pilgrims who need a place to rest."

"Go somewhere else and leave me alone."

"But it is so cold, and we have traveled very far."

"But I do not know you. Who are you?"

"We are Joseph and Mary and our unborn child."

"Then welcome! Please come into our home."

The pilgrims are then received with joy and invited into one another's homes for song and prayer.

Rachel loved this idea and was very excited about it when she described *Las Posadas* to her family that evening. Tom wanted to know how they were going to convince all of the neighbors to buy into it. Peter said he was going to be totally embarrassed if they did anything like it. And Simon, ever the tactful peacemaker, suggested that maybe they could tone it down a little. Rachel was upset that not one of her guys was receptive to the idea. Half-jokingly she called Tom an innkeeper. "Let's give it some more thought," Tom responded gently, not wishing to hurt her feelings any further. Rachel went ahead and, the next day, tried the *Posadas* idea on her neighbor, Holly, who was also a good friend. Holly thought it might be "interesting," which is usually, Rachel knew, a polite code word for "strange." Also Holly reminded Rachel that as long as they had been in this neighborhood, they had never been able to get any sort of holiday gathering organized, let alone one as specific and demanding as this. Rachel gave up on *Las Posadas*.

Feeling that the whole project had fallen on her shoulders alone, Rachel had a serious chat with Tom and told him that if they really wanted to do something more meaningful this year, she was going to need his help. Tom apologized for not being more cooperative and said he would put his thinking cap on full blast over the next day or so. When Tom was finished with his high-power thinking, he confessed that all he could come up with was a simple idea but one that would, he thought, help all of them to enhance their understanding of the great gift of the incarnation. Tom suggested that they adopt a less-fortunate family and give them an entire Christmas. He said that an organization in the city was advertising for people to adopt families in this way. Rachel viewed this as a wonderful idea and told Tom to go ahead and look into adopting a family for Christmas. But she also wanted to do something more—something unconventional.

She went to the source, looking up the story as it is described in the Gospel according to Luke. There Rachel found Joseph and Mary traveling to Bethlehem to complete the registration that had been required of the whole world by the Emperor Augustus. In Bethlehem, Mary gave birth and placed the newborn in a manger because there was no room in the inn. The story unfolded so quickly. Within a matter of a few words, it was accomplished. Enter terrified shepherds and glorious angels bearing good news of great joy. There were amazement and treasuring and pondering and praising. It seemed to Rachel that all of the descriptive material that artists and musicians and theologians and retailers seemed to have at their disposal was missing from this very simply told story. How was she supposed to bring this story to life with so few details? What were the colors, the sounds? What was the *feel* of this story of stories?

One day while the great idea was still waiting to present itself, Holly invited Rachel over for coffee. Holly had three boys, all younger than Peter and Simon. They were evenly spaced two years apart and currently in the first, third, and fifth grades. Holly looked to Rachel, therefore, to provide advice, sanity, and hope. Rachel, who often relied on Holly as a sounding board, reviewed her Advent frustrations, sighing, "I just wish there were some way we could place ourselves in that stable."

"Why don't you?" asked Holly, "I know you can't actually be in that exact stable, but you could all go to a stable. Stay all night if you like! See what it's really like."

Holly was, of course, mostly kidding, but Rachel sort of liked the idea. She did some homework and found a small sheep farm not far from Manassas. She summoned her courage and called the owner of Dorset Farm, a man named Benjamin Lee. She came right out and told him what she was up to and asked whether or not it would be possible for a family to stay there overnight, say on Christmas Eve.

"Aren't you worried about the cold?" he asked.

"It hasn't been too bad. This is Virginia, after all. It could be worse—could be New Hampshire or North Dakota."

There was an extended pause in the conversation in which the puzzled sheep-farm owner was struggling to locate an appropriate response. Rachel jumped in again, saying, "We could pay you." He suggested that payment would not be necessary, but he would need time to think about such an unusual request. Rachel was so excited that the next day, once the kids were on the school bus, she roped Holly into coming with her to see the farm. It was only about a fifteen-mile drive, and it was a stunningly sunny day.

Rachel was always amazed at how quickly the landscape changed from the suburban sprawl surrounding Washington, D.C., to rolling bucolic countryside. It was a beautiful autumn day, not too cold. In fact, to the delight of everyone except snow-seeking youngsters, recent days had been unseasonably warm. They drove through miles of rail-fenced properties on roads that had been major thoroughfares during the Civil War. Then a wooden sign for Dorset Farm directed them to turn onto a very narrow road. After they drove past a thickly wooded area, the sheep pastures suddenly appeared, acres and acres of low grassy hills dotted with grazing sheep. Rachel knew next to nothing about sheep. They were not as white as she expected, and there were, much to her surprise, a couple of black sheep among them. The farm had a large barn and something like a lean-to, only bigger, which was full of hay. "There it is!" she cried. "There's our stable!" Holly, who was at once trying to be supportive and sensible, queried her friend, "Is this something you really want to do?" "Maybe," she said honestly. They did not stop at the farm. Rachel measured on the tachometer approximately one mile's distance from the lean-to to a gas station. They could leave a car parked at the gas station and hike up to the sheep farm. In that way they could experience, in a small way, the holy family's journey on foot. They could bring warm sleeping bags and pack enough food for one night and see what it might have been like.

At home that evening, Rachel described her latest Christmas scheme to three deadpan faces. Tom, from whom she had kept the brilliant idea until this moment, offered a tentative "Novel thought." Peter, speaking in a very measured manner, said, "I think this is going a bit too far, Mom." Simon, mulling it over in his young head, finally added, "Let's do it. It will be like camping out for Christmas."

After a bit of bicker and banter, everyone agreed to think about it for a few days and to do some additional research. Tom suggested that each family member look up one piece of information related to the possible expedition. They were off and running, with varying degrees of enthusiasm.

One week later, the Harrigans gathered for a family meeting. At that time, Tom reminded everyone that they would be adopting a family for Christmas and that any day now, they would be given more information about their family so that they could start shopping. Then they proceeded to what Peter was now calling "Mom's Mad Mutton Scheme." Simon said that he had researched the temperature in Bethlehem at this time of year, which he said would be a little warmer, because Bethlehem was approximately eight degrees latitude south of where they lived in Virginia. It was feasible, he commented, but would not be the same as Bethlehem.

Tom had researched foods suitable to the occasion: Bread, cheese, olives, fruit, and dried fish or meats were the foods of both choice and necessity for Middle Eastern travelers two thousand years ago. Peter said that he had not accomplished any actual study, but that he had thought long and hard about donkey transportation and thought it would be unreasonable to travel in this way. Rachel answered that according to Luke, there were not any donkeys in the story anyway. She proceeded to explain her idea of driving most of the way and walking the final mile. "What about flashlights?" Tom asked. Simon thought that since there were no flashlights back then, they should not use them now. Tom then asked if it would be all right to use his old oil camping lantern, and everyone agreed that oil lanterns had been around for thousands of years, and there was no reason, therefore, not to use it.

Rachel, having done most of the initial footwork on the project, spoke twice more with Benjamin Lee, who finally agreed they could stay in his lean-to as long as they did not make much noise. The dogs, which were very protective of their woolly charges, slept in the house but were very sensitive to nighttime disturbances in the sheep fields. While she had him on the phone, she also inquired about the black sheep, which she had always thought of as nothing more than part of a quaint expression. He told her that the black sheep were as much a part of the flock as the white. There was a recessive gene that created the black sheep, which, in contrast to the expression, were valued for their unique coats.

Rachel and Simon were growing more and more ambitious in their plans, but Tom's reservations seemed to be growing, and Peter's disdain for the project was reaching explosive proportions. A few days before Christmas, Peter announced that he was not going. He would rather spend Christmas Eve all by himself than out in some sheep field surrounded by stupid, messy animals. Rachel tried to reassure him, but he was resolute in his objections. Everyone but Peter continued their sheep-farm preparations. Peter agreed to concentrate on the family they were adopting for Christmas.

It was a small family—a single mom with two young children, a boy and a girl. The family description arrived with a list of items that they would like for Christmas. Most of the desired items were clothing: a coat for the little boy, a sweater for his mother, warm pants and socks for everyone. The extras were nonspecific: a doll, a truck, a hair dryer—"any kind, does not need to be new." Peter looked through the Sunday paper for specials. With a big red marker, he circled items that fit the bill and were also on sale. Then he created a list based on his discoveries. While he was not prepared to make any contribution to "Mom's Mad Mutton Scheme," he felt he could share in this year's Christmas by getting the adopt-a-family program organized. Using his lists, Rachel and Peter went shopping for their adopted family. She tried to offer him encouragement and expressed her gratitude for his help.

On the day before Christmas Eve, Tom and Simon went grocery shopping and came home with bottles of spring water, a box of pitted dates, two sizable hunks of mild cheese, four great big loaves of hearty fresh-baked bread, a big package of shrink-wrapped meat sticks, and a can of black olives. There were several different choices of gourmet olives in the deli section, for which Tom campaigned, but his youngest son convinced him that while everyone in the family enjoyed ordinary canned black olives, only two of the family members would be the slightest bit interested in the gourmet variety.

On the morning of Christmas Eve, the Harrigans gathered up the packages they had wrapped for their adopted family and placed them in a big red cotton sack that Rachel made just for this special delivery. They found everything on their adopted family's Christmas wish list and added a few extras, too: a canned ham, a small bag of potatoes, and a box of fat candy canes. These they delivered to a community center that was handling collection and distribution. The boys were disappointed that they did not get to meet the children for whom they had shopped, but a very nice man at the community center explained how much their gifts would be appreciated. Looking at the great piles of gifts already gathered, Peter thought about how many families had so little.

The Harrigans ate their big meal in the middle of the day so that they would not be too hungry for the journey. Peter and Simon emptied their backpacks of schoolbooks and loose papers and repacked them with food and supplies. Sleeping bags were rolled securely, and the oil lantern was prepared. Peter had decided that while he still objected to the whole idea, he was willing to come along with his family to the sheep farm—if only to prove to his mother what a worthless experience it would be.

Departure time was eight o'clock, prior to which they ate a hearty snack of chowder and grilled cheese sandwiches. Their stomachs well prepared, off they went. Everything looked very different in the dark than it had looked when Rachel and Holly had first come to scope out the location. They left the car at the gas station, which was now closed for the holiday. Tom lit the oil lantern, and they all hiked in the direction of the sheep farm. It was a beautiful night, cold but still, and there was very little traffic on the road. The three or four cars that did pass by made Simon wonder aloud what they thought of a family wandering along a country road on Christmas Eve. "Do you think they think we are homeless?" he asked. The boys carried the backpacks, Tom carried the lantern and a small bag full of hats and gloves and dry socks. Rachel had tied all of the sleeping bags together and had these slung over her back. After a while, she and Tom traded loads.

The mile went very quickly, which made Rachel think she should have stretched out the journey. Nevertheless, she was glad to be there and looked forward to settling in for the night in their uncommon quarters. Benjamin Lee and three of his border collies met the Harrigans on his front porch. "Nice-looking family," he said. "You sure you want to go through with this?" Peter nobly kept his mouth shut as his father answered, "Yes, and thank you very much for this enormous favor." Ben Lee reminded the Harrigans to be as quiet as they could out there so as not to rouse the dogs. He told them to watch where they stepped as they went out to the lean-to and not to worry about the sheep. "They're quite dumb, you know," he said in the confidence that comes with experience.

The Harrigans managed to sidestep their way through the well-fertilized pasture to the "stable." Benjamin Lee had prepared it for them with fresh, sweet-smelling hay, which made up slightly for the unavoidable smell of the flock. None of them had, until this moment, ever thought about how the stable might have smelled. "Remember," said Tom, "they didn't have deodorant back then, either. After a long trip like that, it wasn't just the animals that smelled." They fashioned a sleeping area in the hay and set out the bags. They did not have highly insulated sleeping bags back in Bethlehem, but they did use blankets and down feathers; the family had agreed, therefore, that sleeping bags were perfectly allowable. They settled into them and began to allow the sights and sounds and smells to surround them.

It was a clear moonless night, and the stars were exceptionally bright. Simon pointed to a brilliant star which Peter identified as Betelgeuse, in the constellation Orion. They marveled over the challenge of using the stars as directional signals the way the Magi had. They were surprised at the quietness of the sleeping sheep scattered in little bundles across the field. Without the usual sounds of traffic and the television, they remarked on the silence of the night, which did indeed create a sense of holiness. They nibbled on bread and cheese and dates and spent the night in awe-filled, whispered wonderings, which led to a peaceful and fairly comfortable sleep in the hay.

Early Christmas morning, the Harrigans awoke to the sound of barking dogs. Holly and her husband and three children had decided to play the part of the Magi and bring the poor Harrigans breakfast gifts of golden crullers and hot spiced cider. "We couldn't find any myrrh," Holly explained. The two families sat in the sweet hay on that crisp December morning enjoying their breakfast gifts and one another's company.

"So how did it go?" asked Holly.

Tom answered first. "I was prepared for the worst," he said, "but I think we all have a better idea of Bethlehem now."

"It really was a magnificent night," Rachel added.

Simon nodded in agreement while dabbing his runny nose with his shirt sleeve. Peter sat in an unreadable silence, offering no clear response.

Then Simon's once reluctant soul admitted, "I think Jesus was closer to God outside in a manger than he would have been inside anyway." And there it was—the moment for which Rachel and Tom had been hoping.

Once they were back home in the warm safety and familiar noise of their own home, there would be other gifts exchanged that

Christmas morning. None, however, would be as lovely as the gift expressed in Simon's simple words about Jesus: "I think Jesus was closer to God outside in a manger than he would have been inside anyway." His words expressed a glimpse of the divine, an experience of the holy, a step into the sacred story, a step up in the mysterious journey of faith.

Questions for Reflection and Discussion

1. The Harrigans wanted to bring the Christmas story to life. Did they succeed?
2. If Rachel had been able to find the kind of nativity set for which she initially searched, would its presence in the Harrigan living room have produced the effect she desired?
3. What do you think of *Las Posadas?* Could it happen in your neighborhood?
4. Mothers are often expected to manage the religious life of a family. In what ways have you seen this happen? Is this fair?
5. Why were Tom and Peter so resistant, at first, to Rachel's sheep-farm idea?
6. Which was the more important celebration of the incarnation, adopting a family for Christmas or staying overnight on the sheep farm? Why?
7. What do you think was the most spiritual aspect of the Harrigans' farm adventure?
8. Do you think the Harrigans will repeat this experience? Would you? Do you have other ideas for bringing the Christmas story to life?

Scripture Index